Switch on your IoT
Preparing for tomorrow's business

AUTHOR René Wiersma
COMMISSIONED BY Yenlo
WITH CONTRIBUTIONS FROM John Mathon, Paul Fremantle and Ruben van der Zwan
EDITOR Inge de Jong, Heuvel Marketing
DESIGN AND LAY-OUT Ivo van IJzendoorn, IvoGraphics

Printed by CreateSpace
Available on Amazon and through other online stores

The original study was conducted in collaboration with and
coordinated by the Nyenrode Business University, The Netherlands.

SWITCH ON YOUR IOT

Preparing for tomorrow's business

– René Wiersma –

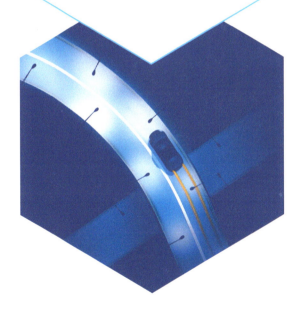

Yenlo.

Table of Contents

1. ▸ What do you have to do with all of this?

So the Internet of Things is a big deal. But how do you turn it into something of value? And who do you need to get the job done? Even more important: why should you want to get the job done anyway? Why do you, of all people, need to get on board? Well, here is what we think. You did not come across this book by accident. Someone must have given it to you, knowing you are interested in this subject. And if they did not, you must have picked it up yourself, because the title and images caught your attention. Either way, you are suited to read this book, simply because you have an eye for opportunity. Where others would have sighed while thinking: "Let's not go there, let's not dream big", you think the complete opposite. And that is all you need to switch on your IoT: ambition, a vision, and a bit of courage. And a business, that will come in handy too.

So, no more doubts about whether you are the man or woman for the job, because you are. And you will not have to do it all by yourself; as specialists in the domain of cool IT stuff, we will guide you through the entire process. Now let us get to it, we want to be innovators, not laggards!

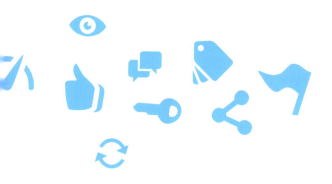

 "Ambition,

a vision,

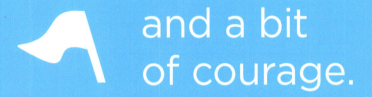 and a bit of courage.

That is all you need to take IoT to the next level"

2. ▸ Foreword by Ruben van der Zwan

Ruben van der Zwan is CEO and co-founder of Yenlo. More than ten years ago, he started Yenlo to deliver top-shelf IT consultancy services based on true craftsmanship in the field of API, IoT and SOA centric environments. He is a true open source evangelist and uses the technology to deliver tailor-made solutions to businesses all around the world. He shares his vision, knowledge and pragmatic approach at many international conferences, often as a keynote speaker.

A brilliant idea always starts with one crazy person, whether this person is an explorer, a scientist, or a software architect. They are assumed to be insane until their idea becomes a great success, and then they are suddenly hailed as heroes. This is the fate of many great thinkers, discoverers, and yes, software vendors who want to disrupt their business.

At Yenlo, we love crazy people. Not just because they are fun (they are), but because being crazy always pays off in the end. I remember me and my business partner Maarten de Waal started out with nothing but a wild plan. We wanted to change the software industry by integrating and connecting everything that could possibly be integrated and connected. Did we have any idea what we had gotten ourselves into? We did not have a clue. Our crazy idea worked out well, though, and today Yenlo is the home of many bright and curious minds, who bring change to more than just the software industry.

So when René Wiersma came to my office in 2011 to tell me he wanted to go back to university for his Executive MBA degree, I cheered. Not because I was happy to see him leave, but because I believe in people that take a leap. It got even better last year, when René told me he was planning on writing a master thesis on the Internet of Things and its possible added value to businesses like ours. We sat down and talked for a little while. I realized René was onto something: IoT had become a trending topic, and all sorts of businesses had started using IoT techniques to improve their products and services. Many of them, some of them being our very own customers, had already turned to us for help. Clearly, our knowledge on integration software had made us a key player in their IoT story. Clearly, we had a story to tell.

"Why aren't we anticipating on this?" we asked ourselves, and five minutes later, it was settled. René would be writing his master thesis on the Internet of Things, and he would simultaneously explore ways for us to add value to our business. It fitted perfectly into our R&D driven strategy and the Yenlo LABS department, the place where we explore crazy ideas on a technological level. Yenlo would become René's proud sponsor and I would be closely monitoring the entire process. And then things started to happen. We got into contact with many interesting people who have worked or have started with IoT projects, and who would gladly share their success stories and even their failures. They told us all about relevant business building blocks, key competences, and main challenges that are associated with IoT projects. Halfway through the project, René and I realized we would be mad if we did not share their stories with the world. So we came up with an even crazier plan, and turned the thesis into a book. The very one that you are reading right now.

> "Why aren't we anticipating on this?" we asked ourselves, and five minutes later, it was settled.

This book is based on the thesis that René wrote, however, we challenged ourselves to provide you with a couple of extras. That is why we called in the help of two heavy weights in the integration software industry. I am, of course, referring to none other than **John Mathon**, co-founder of TIBCO and currently Vice President of Strategy at Yenlo, and **Paul Fremantle,** co-founder of WSO2 and currently doing a PHD in the Internet of Things at the University of Plymouth. Both of them were so kind to take the time to share their interesting stories and hand them over to us. In the next chapter, John Mathon will share his vision on IoT and its power to change your business. Paul Fremantle is featured in chapter 7, in which he will tell you all about his reference architecture, which you can use as a framework for your future IoT projects.

In 2011, all we had was an idea. Now, we have an Executive MBA graduate, a thesis, a book, many interesting stories, and even more new insights into the value of IoT for software vendors. I believe that your business in IoT will work the same way; you need to come up with something completely new and unique, and you have to get the right people on board and learn from them.

So go ahead. Read this book, and be that crazy person.

Ruben van der Zwan
CEO and co-founder of Yenlo

▸Foreword by John Mathon 3.

John Mathon is one of the founders of TIBCO where he served as CTO for 15 years. He has been Vice President of Computer Associates and in 2013 he became Vice President Product Strategy at WSO2. In 2016, John Mathon joined Yenlo as Vice President of Strategy. He invented the publish/subscribe pattern and has 10+ patents in messaging, security, content management, and file systems. John Mathon is a well-known keynote speaker at universities and international conferences.

IoT is all about smart solutions. Take the example of Publish/Subscribe (PubSub), a messaging pattern I invented. This idea used widely enables us to easily share information with everyone who is interested, without having to know who the subscribers to the information are. This sharing is done automatically so I do not have to send individual messages to all the subscribers. Almost all IoT devices talk using PubSub. If one device has a problem, other devices can provide information redundantly or make up for the failure instantly and seamlessly.

This form of intelligence is what we are looking for in our IoT solutions whether for the consumer or the business. It is the key benefit IoT can bring over individual devices. By working together using PubSub, devices can communicate and operate in concert to provide added value, resulting in amazing applications. Imagine a heart sensor that is tied to your cell phone, which can trigger immediate response in an emergency, provides feedback on the time to arrival, gives advice to help the patient before they arrive, and which notifies any nearby trained personnel!

> "When deployed well, IoT has the ability to change the world"

IoT applications pop up everywhere and get adopted by organizations and institutions all around the world. The US military, for instance, is spending a billion dollars on IoT devices to monitor military personnel in the field. Health organizations develop applications that can measure glucose levels dynamically as well as other vital signs allowing much faster response to medical situations. Another great example of a really well integrated IoT device I love is my Tesla. The Tesla has the ability to download new versions of itself over time, a degree of cleverness any IoT device should have to improve itself. It is such a great concept that things improve with time rather than degrade! Imagine if everything could improve with time, self-report problems and even fix themselves. When deployed well, IoT has the ability to change the world.

But how exactly does IoT create value to your business? Let us stick with the Tesla example. The car captures data from the operation of the car to detect parts that are not operating as well. It can tell if a part needs to be replaced before you are even aware of it and way before you take it in for service. Tesla uses this information not only to provide you with better service, but also to optimize their products by buying components from a different manufacturer or design something differently that affects the next car made on the factory floor. By constantly gathering data from their cars, Tesla is able to modify their offerings more rapidly and reduce recall notices or customer dissatisfaction. The results are stunning, as Tesla has 98% to 99% customer satisfaction in surveys for all the years it has been making cars. Commitment to quality and being responsive and proactive clearly produces loyalty.

"Imagine if everything could improve with time, self-report problems and even fix themselves"

IoT applications thus contribute to customer satisfaction and loyalty. But I believe Tesla has achieved more than just that. The company has disrupted the entire car industry with the IoT Connected Car, even more than the electric vehicle did. Virtually every car manufacturer has announced that new cars in the next year or two will be IoT connected Cars. IoT Cars are expected to be a large portion of the trillions of dollars spent on IoT, possibly as much as 30% in the early years. By deploying IoT, Tesla has conquered the car industry and is on top of every single form of car innovation. In other words: IoT worked out pretty well for them.

Creating this magical world of intelligent IoT devices that work together and provide intelligence is not easy. Your IoT implementations need to collect data from devices and this has to be studied to determine how best to benefit your company. Moreover, consumer IoT and Industrial IoT (IIoT) are not the same thing and call for different approaches. The two markets have divergent requirements and competencies to be successful. Consumer devices need to focus on appealing design and ease of use. Industrial IoT devices, on the other hand, need to be robust, reliable, secure, and they have to come with APIs to do custom integration.

Let us look at some requirements for industrial IoT applications. A key element of IIoT is security. Some companies may not be able to either build or use IoT devices until they can solve their security issues. Security is composed of authentication, authorization and audit. Each aspect of security is hard and requires domain expertise. Many IoT devices are deficient in security and need expert help to produce secure solutions. In many cases, IoT security needs to be combined and integrated with other security systems in corporations. Device Management is a new application for IoT and is just starting to be available to provide powerful security tools.

One security issue that is widely unsolved is authentication. A new technology called PUF (Physical Unclonable Function, a function that cannot be duplicated and therefore lowers security risks) may be a long term solution but is not available generally yet. Managing large numbers of IoT devices whether in the home or office is difficult. UMA (User-Managed Access) is a security standard that is just emerging that could provide policy based security and privacy control. Encryption, a basic requirement is not standard in all devices. Another big hole is that most devices do not automatically upgrade or are difficult to keep up to date with the latest security patches. Yet another difficulty is created by completely different protocols between different devices and the cloud, making integration harder than it should be. Vendors still operate as if their devices were the only devices you will ever work with or buy. Industry or product standardization of protocols, security and integration does not exist yet and requires customization for every manufacturer.

"In my opinion, employing an ISV is an ideal way of overcoming security issues"

Both IoT and IIoT need integration as a critical capability. For the consumer the integration has to be really simple. Industrial applications need a data infrastructure to collect and distribute data to different tiers. Industrial users will want to mine the information to detect ways to improve their business efficiency and find intelligence in the data to produce opportunities. They will want to find ways to create value related to their individual company.

In my opinion, employing an ISV (Independent Software Vendor) is an ideal way of overcoming the aforementioned security issues, integration issues, data mining and intelligence. Some ISVs have specific industry or application expertise. There are ISVs to help you build applications for energy efficiency or to build scalable cloud solutions using IoT devices. Achieving "intelligent IoT devices" is harder than it seems. ISVs with IoT experience therefore can play an important role in leveraging IoT to produce value for the supplier and the consumer.

Since most issues that come with deploying IoT can be solved by involving a specialized ISV, there is nothing standing in your way of developing your very own IoT applications. And in contrast to many other business opportunities, the benefits of IoT are twofold. With IoT devices and applications, we add value to our company offerings while building a smarter world with less mistakes made and integrated behavior that really saves time, money, and makes our lives better. How? We will tell you all about it in this book. You better start reading!

John Mathon
Vice President of Strategy at Yenlo

▶ Introduction

4.

Multinational Boeing connects on-board applications with repair services at the airport, minimizing downtime and maximizing flight hours[1]. Smart thermostats keep you up to date on the state of all your household appliances, lowering utility expenses and growing environmental awareness. Taxi service Uber is just around the corner, but you have been tracking the car for miles on your smartphone. Situations like these are no pie in the sky; they are happening as we speak.

- By 2020 the Internet of Things (IoT) will include 26 billion units, and by that time, IoT product and service suppliers will generate incremental revenue exceeding $300 billion, mostly in services[2]

- In 2022 1 trillion sensors will be connected to the Internet[3]

"People start to realize IoT could potentially transform industries and the way we live and work"

Something is going on, and it has been going on for a while now. Mankind has dreamt of the future forever, which we hoped would be filled with exciting inventions, such as talking objects and trips to Mars. Those dreams never came true, and we were disappointed until we decided to give up and to get back to our daily lives. We turned our concept of what we hoped would be our future into animated movies for children and rested our case. In the meantime, we kept on developing cool things, but we never really dared to go beyond existing technologies. Up until now. With the rise of the Internet of Things (IoT), our wildest fantasies about an exciting future have found their way back into our heads and hearts,

---

1   WSO2, (Feb 13, 2014) **"How Boeing Transformed Commercial Aviation Using WSO2"**.
2   Gartner, (2014a). **"Gartner Says the Internet of Things Will Transform the Data Center"**.
3   Global Agenda Council on the Future of Software & Society, (2015).

as we start to realize it could potentially transform industries and the way we live and work. At the heart of the concept lies the idea that objects – things – are capable of processing information, communicating with each other and with their environment, and autonomous decision taking[4]. So today, objects actually do talk and seem to be living an autonomous life, while making our lives easier, safer, and more comfortable at the same time. Where does all of this come from? Did IoT turn up out of the blue? Or did we have something to do with it? Did the technical world impose IoT on us, or are we part of the movement? The latter seems to be true. People like you and me are the inspiration that boosted the popularity of IoT, and pushed developers to create amazing things. There is no need to be afraid of technology, as we ourselves are the force behind it.

Schiphol airport installed two thousand beacons that assist passengers and staff that navigate through the terminal. They also developed a digital boarding pass, that makes it unnecessary for travellers to bring a printed copy. Schiphol owns the beacons, but the network is open to shops, hotels, and airline companies.[5]

Are we ready?

There is a reason all of this is happening today instead of twenty years ago. Back then, many enthusiasts dreamt big about IoT and its possibilities. They wanted to provide every single person, object, and device with identifiers, so they could exchange data with each other, businesses and maybe even the government. During the 1990s, Radio-frequency identification (RFID)[6] was deemed most suitable to facilitate this interaction and the technique was therefore used to transport the information. The problem was that back then people were not ready for such a break-through. The thought of being chipped, followed, and monitored in all of their movements horrified the public and made it reject any kind of collaboration. Getting involved in an international network of data exchange would be taking ten steps back in terms of freedom and

---

4 Uckelmann, D., Harrison, M., & Michahelles, F. (2011). **Architecting the Internet of Things.**
5 iBeaconinfo. (2015, July 16). **Schiphol heeft bijna 2000 beacons geplaatst.**
   Retrieved November 1, 2015, from iBeaconinfo.
6 Balamuralidhar, P., Prateep, M., & Arpan, P. (2013). **Software Platforms for Internet of Things and M2M.**

self-determination. Moreover, work and private lives were kept separate, remote work was not an option and new communication technologies were not fine-tuned to the users' needs. People were not ready, neither was technology. RFID, although pretty revolutionary at the time, did not add value to daily life, customer experience or business development. Privacy could not be guaranteed[7], software was too complex and expensive for small business owners, and the possibility of electromagnetic radiance did not exactly contribute to the adoption of IoT by society.

Macy's, the well-known department store in the USA, deployed shopkick's ShopBeacon technology, an innovative mobile location-based technology that uses ultrasound Bluetooth Low Energy. ShopBeacon provides app users with personalized department-level deals, discounts, recommendations, and rewards.[8]

Embracing technology

It is abundant to say that things have changed. The internet was integrated in the business world and our private lives, blurring the line between work and leisure, national and international communication, and small business owners and multinationals. The omnipresence of the internet has lowered entry barriers, and pushes startups with brilliant ideas to rise to great heights. Today, you do not need to spend a fortune on hardware, offices, devices, and paper. Today, all you need to get started is a website, and they are practically for free. Smartphones have taken over the world and have made us flexible, as we can do business when and wherever we want. We no longer mind planning our meetings in coffee houses, or checking our work inbox at the dinner table. Our jobs have become part of our private lives, and we gladly work from home on Saturdays so we can sleep until noon on Mondays. In other words: people have embraced technology and they use it to make their lives easier and more fun. They are no longer scared of losing the important things in life, such as human interaction, culture and art,

---

7 Albrecht, K. (2008). **How RFID Tags Could Be Used to Track Unsuspecting People.**
8 Lee, I., & Lee, K. (2015). **The Internet of Things (IoT): Applications, investments, and challenges for enterprises.** Business Horizons, 58, 431-440.

to the online world; instead they find ways to add value to these matters, by combining the virtual with the natural. People are ready for the next step, whereas in the nineties, they were not.

Gartner Hype cycle

Looking at this forecast from a commercial perspective, we believe many salesmen cannot wait to take their piece of the cake. IoT is catching on fast in all parts of the world, and many believe that now is the time to start and take a stab at a leading position in their branch. The latest reports on the position of IoT in the Gartner hype cycle[9] seem to agree. This cycle represents the emergence, adoption, maturity, and impact on applications of specific technologies, and IoT reached the "Peak of Inflated Expectations" and was forecasted to take five to ten years for market adoption. Nevertheless, the "Trough of Disillusionment" is lurking, meaning that the bright future of IoT is not yet guaranteed. Obviously, there are obstacles to overcome, such as privacy and security. The greater the impact of IoT, the greater the impact of security breaches. Issues like power cuts, black hat hackers, and data leakage could cause serious problems and harm both organizations and people. Think about the cyber-attack that disabled a great part of Ukraine in 2015[10]! Not to mention the distrust of new technologies that would follow after serious

9   Gartner. (n.d.). **Gartner Hype Cycle.** http://www.gartner.com/technology/research/
    methodologies/hype-cycle.jsp
10 **Hackers caused power cut in western Ukraine - US. (2016, January 12). Retrieved June 24, 2016,
    from http://www.bbc.co.uk/news/technology-35297464**

incidents and privacy scandals. Moreover, despite the enormous forecasted potentials of IoT, many organizations do not know how to get started and what it takes to make actual money with it. They might not dispose of the crucial but complex technologies that are needed in order to implement IoT in a business. When it comes to innovation, having a great idea is not enough. Ideas need to get implemented with the right expertise, by the right people that have the right experience. Only then a business stands a chance in our fast growing and competitive society.

"Ideas need to get implemented with the right expertise, by the right people that have the right experience"

Then there was Tesla

As it turns out, some businesses have already found ways to turn IoT into revenue. Suddenly Tesla was here, the much discussed electric car and ultimate IoT example[11]. Being non-stop connected to Wi-Fi and Bluetooth, the vehicle exchanges data to perform automatic updates and to communicate driving behavior and possible defects. This way, Tesla developers have direct insight into usage patterns, power consumption, and the state of the car itself, which allows them to optimally adapt their services and software. By doing this, Tesla Motors ensures that drivers will no longer have to undertake time consuming trips to the garage for maintenance, check-ups, and updates. Tesla Motors is the living proof of the added value that can be created with IoT, as the benefits are two-fold: the Tesla owner drives a fully equipped car that offers extra services and contributes to user comfort; the company uses the insights they gain from the data to maximize customer satisfaction and to raise sales. But they are not alone in their success. Dutch developer Quby launched a smart thermostat[12] that connects to smartphones and tablets through an app, allowing users to not just manage and lower their energy consumption, but also to connect to apps from external developers. This way, something as simple as a thermostat changes into a household manager, communicating with washing machines, smoke detectors and oth

11 Brisbourne, A. (n.d.). **Tesla's Over-the-Air Fix: Best Example Yet of the Internet of Things?**
12 Quby. (n.d.). **Smart thermostat,** http://quby.com/en/page/62

er devices such as lamps and fridges. This shows the true power of IoT: thanks to its technology, people can use every day devices to create a network of services that offer more value together than one device could ever effectuate.

"People do not want to be told what to do; they want comfort, opportunities and freedom"

Why are we so eager to connect?

Where does this desperate need to connect come from? Why do people need their smartphones to tell them their laundry can be taken out of the washing machine? Why do they need their vehicles to remind them of their next business meeting? The truth is, they do not. Consumers would be just fine waiting for their laundry, hanging around at the office waiting for their next meeting without the Internet of Things connecting them to their devices. But that is not the point. People have a tendency to improve, to solve and to change. The world as we know it goes round, but they are determined to make it go round in a smoother way. Better. Faster. People do not want to be slaves to their job and households; they want their devices to take away everything that keeps them from living a happy life. Business men and women refuse to drown in enormous amounts of administration, schedules, and useless business meetings at the office, and they choose to go out for a coffee instead. At the coffee place, they will check their email and make some phone calls, but only in the way they prefer. They do not want to be told what to do; they want comfort, opportunities and freedom. If this means having to share their whereabouts, preferences, and personal details, so be it. Now that IT is ready to turn desire into reality, people get more impatient by the second.

Living Labs, a collaboration between the city council of Amsterdam, entrepreneurs, and developers, is working on an interactive and innovative city. The organization placed iBeacons and IoT enabled smart beacons that communicate over LoRa (Long Range), which is a Low Power Wide Area Network (LPWAN), across several hotspots in the capital city. This way, Living Labs aims to stimulate innovative start-ups, entrepreneurs, and SMEs across public and private industry sectors, leading to better interaction with citizens, entrepreneurs, and visitors.[13]

Putting IoT to work

That is not all though. IoT goes beyond the boundaries of consumerism and realizes change in several components of our lives. By integrating IoT in hospitals, classrooms, and even in a cowshed, essential improvements can be made that have a positive impact on our health and personal development, environmental protection, and quality of life in general. Again, not by throwing money at it, but by taking something simple -yet essential- and to integrate it with other things so networks get created that add value through all the data they produce. Sounds good, yet abstract, right? Let us zoom into some examples. In the paragraphs below, we will have a look at three main fields of IoT, which are healthcare, education, and agriculture.

> "IoT saves out on time, man power and costs by using that what is already there"

High hopes for healthcare

Let us take a look at the medical world first. Due to the many different healthcare organizations, insurance companies, authorities, and cuts in health budgets, this world has turned into a true labyrinth in which communication and personal care leave much to be desired. The amount of paper work, the many people in

---

13 **Amsterdam iBeacon Living Lab.** Retrieved November 1, 2015, from iBeacon Living Lab: http://ibeaconlivinglab.com/ For more information on LoRa, see the LoRa Alliance website: https://www.lora-alliance.org/

volved, and the increased work load of caregivers stand in the way of patient differentiation, quality improvement, and, yes, innovation. When integrating IoT with healthcare, these major issues can be tackled. As a matter of fact, some of the issues are being dealt with right at the very moment you are reading this book; think about it. Patient information systems[14] are being integrated in the cloud, online portals are being installed to connect clients with their doctors, while new medical devices collect and analyze data and keep a close eye on the wellbeing of their patients twenty-four hours a day. So instead of injecting money into the health healthcare sector, IoT saves out on time, manpower and costs by using that what is already there -people, medical staff, devices, and paperwork- and connecting it to everyone and everything involved, resulting in less workload, more cost savings, better healthcare, more safety, and eventually a higher quality of life.

Schools and robots

But what about education? Should we fear robots taking over classrooms, resulting in scholars that do not know how to interact with actual people and forget how to write, head count, and collaborate? Fortunately, we do not. IoT realizes the exact opposite, as it enables teachers to provide their students with personalized tasks, support, and feedback[15]. Look at Google Glass[16], for example. This device can be put to work as a personal teacher, as it measures the reading speed and common pitfalls of the user. All the data it collects, will be sent to an online database, which makes it easier for teachers to monitor the progress of their students. Even better; data from several schools can get analyzed and benchmarked, resulting in more insights into the quality of education per school and the learning patterns of students. And do not forget about smartphones. Schools seem to be unable to ban them from the classroom, so they might as well put them to good use. You might think IoT is a total distraction from schoolwork, however, it can transform a student's phone into a helpful learning tool, turning exercises into competitive games, while constantly communicating with fellow students and teachers. Furthermore, smartphones could be used as absence detectors, sending signals directly to a teacher's smartphone. This may sound futuristic;

---

14 **A guide to healthcare IoT possibilities and obstacles.** (n.d.). http://searchhealthit. techtarget.com/essentialguide/A-guide-to-healthcare-IoT-possibilities-and-obstacles

15 Wielen, G., van der. (2016, February 5). **Interview with IoT experts** [Interview by R. Wiersma].

16 Afshar, V. (2014, May 29). **14 Google Glass Innovative Uses In Education.** http://www.huffingtonpost.com/vala-afshar/14-google-glass-innovativ_b_5410893.html

many of these applications have already proven their value and are being introduced at schools all around the world. They do not only improve the quality of our children's education; they also put back the fun in the classroom.

Tagging cows

Healthcare and education are essential for a better world, and so is agriculture. Sadly, animal welfare, pollution, and the world economy have not proven to be very compatible. The overproduction of milk lowers prices and increases foreign competition, intensive farming does not benefit the wellbeing of cows, and organic livestock production is a serious soil pollutant[17]. There is a lot at stake when it comes to our daily dairy products, since people, animals, and the environment are involved. This is why some of us have joined forces to develop new farming methods that benefit both farmers and animals, consumers, and nature by using IoT. In a northern province of the Netherlands, for example, researchers from the Wageningen University have founded a true dairy campus, which they use to optimize milk production in a safe, eco-friendly, and efficient way[18]. In order to do so, they look for ways to collect data by placing ID-tags and sensors in and around cows, that monitor their nutrition, health, and milk production. The information they gather will be used to provide each individual cow with the right amount of cattle feed, to signal and cure diseases in good time, and to closely monitor their milk production. These data can be used to micro manage a whole livestock, saving time, money, and manpower. The dairy campus may seem like a small project; it is a real life example of what agriculture will look like in the near future. By gathering information about the actual cattle feed consumption, milk production, and health of each member of the livestock, farmers learn how to adapt their procurement strategy, milking procedures, and scale to get a maximum profit out of their business. At the same time, less cattle feed will go to waste, less milk will be spilled, and less cows are needed to make a living, which reduces the amount of harmful substances in the earth atmosphere. This way, everybody wins.

[17] **Present day dilemmas and problems - Dutch Farm Experience.** (n.d.). http://www.dutchfarm-experience.com/present-day-dillemas-problems/

[18] **Smart Farming (Slim boeren).** (n.d.). http://www.dairycampus.nl/nl/Home/Expertisegebieden/Smart-Farming.htm

"ISVs that know how to capitalize IoT have everything it takes to develop a value network that creates a win-win situation for all stakeholders"

ISVs, your time has come

Looking at the rapid growth of IoT applications, IoT is expected to become an important source of revenue soon[19]. Why? Well, basically because IoT creates billions of new services and products to sell. Businesses that know how to productize their IoT applications create value for other businesses and the consumer market, generating more sales, higher customer satisfaction, and eventually more financial returns. However, since Gartner[20] predicts most IoT related revenue will be generated through services, organizations need to develop new types of business models to ever make it that far. That is why, in this story, Independent Software Vendors play an important role. The term ISV covers all organizations that are specialized in developing and selling software, designed for both mass and niche markets[21]. Being integrators and processors to their bone marrow, ISVs have access to the knowledge, experience, and expertise that is needed to couple different systems and get them to communicate and exchange data in a safe and reliable way. But that is not all. ISVs using IoT have the power to revolutionize market research, as they are able to increase sample sizes, reduce costs of information collection and provide instant feedback by using real-time analytics. In other words, ISVs that know how to capitalize IoT have everything it takes to develop a value network that creates a win-win situation for all stakeholders.

No IoT without a business model

So, many lives are to be improved, wishes are to be fulfilled, and chances are to be taken. However, all the opportunities mentioned above do not grasp themselves. Innovation, and therefore IoT, only works when smart people come up with solid business

---

19 Dijkman, R., Sprenkels, B., Peeters, T., & Janssen, A. (2015). **Business models for the Internet of Things.**

20 Gartner, (2014a). "**Gartner Says the Internet of Things Will Transform the Data Center**".

21 Popp, K., & Meyer, R. (2010). **Profit from Software Ecosystems: Business Models, Ecosystems and Partnerships in the Software Industry.**

models which will turn good ideas into profitable activities. This may sound like a boundary to you; it is actually a great opportunity. In business terms, it means there are thousands of ways for ISVs to put IoT into use and to take the lead with their organization. Not by taking more money from their customers, but by adding value to their products and services, so they, in turn, contribute to the comfort, wellbeing, education, and safety of their own customers. ISVs can make these positive outcomes work for them by building long lasting customer relationships and a strong reputation as an IT innovator. That is pretty awesome on its own; you are allowed to dream even bigger. In the long term, your company can use IoT to create a hub for all your services, setting up a network with partners, clients, and external developers. Just like Tesla partnered up with streaming services like Spotify, battery manufacturer Panasonic, and many others, you can team up with other initiators and make great things happen. All you need is a good idea, great people and, inevitably, a great business model.

"Innovation, no matter how brilliant, should never be used to show off or to be put into use just "because we can"

Classic pitfalls

This great business model, or better put, the lack of it, is the reason why IoT has not conquered the business world just yet. Business owners often do not have the knowledge, ideas, or right partners to take their business to the next level. Technology never ceases to amaze us, but its ambiguity also confuses us. In the absence of people with the right expertise and experience level, their ideas will not make it through the next board meeting. And even if they think they have figured it all out from a technical point of view, they might miss some important matters, like many other enthusiastic business owners have done in the past. Innovation, no matter how brilliant, should never be used to show off or to be put into use just "because we can". Companies that want to innovate often get carried away by the endless possibilities that come with new technologies and inventions, but tend to forget that they should serve a higher purpose. They mistake means for end goals, forget to structure their plans, and take risky side effects of their inventions for granted. Think about something innocent as a smart fridge that knows when it needs a refill. When your fridge knows you are away on holiday, so might hackers with bad intentions, meaning your house might be plundered because of your own household devices. As an ISV, pointing out these risks to your customers is essential when you want to build sustainable IoT solutions. Moreover, you and your customer should think about the actual added value your appliances offer to the end user. In the end, it all comes down to that one question: what does he get out of it? If the answer is "Well, nothing, but it makes us look good", you are doomed to fail.

Time for some action
The opportunities are clear, and so are the obstacles. It is time to find out what IoT can bring and what you need to get you there. That is why we have conducted a thorough research on the subject, exploring technological requirements, main challenges, key competences and possible business models that you should know about when integrating IoT in your business activities. We spoke with experts and practitioners in multiple sectors, both national and international focused, and dove into a pile of studies conducted by other researchers. All our findings are integrated in this book, to make sure that you know about the what, and also about the why and how. In the next chapters, we will tell you how to prepare for tomorow's business in IoT; its pitfalls and requirements and of course the success stories of our interviewees. In the final chapters, we will provide you with specific recommendations, giving you insights into the ultimate software architecture, the ultimate challenges, the ultimate competences and, last but not least, the ultimate business model for a business in IoT.

It is time to pass on our knowledge and study findings and get you on the right track. A track that will most certainly lead you to new business opportunities, better customer experience, and, eventually, higher revenue.

Enjoy!

"When it comes
to innovation,
having a great
idea is not enough"

5. ► What do you need to know?

Although market research agencies predict a glorious future for IoT applications, it does not appear that many ISVs really made the shift towards a successful commercial exploitation just yet. So what problems do they encounter when starting with IoT? The truth is that organizations often do not know where or how to start[22]. IoT is all about integration and it highly relies on interdependencies, meaning there is a lot to it. The company will need knowledge, expertise, experience, and most important of all, a network. ISVs starting with IoT need to understand how others in the ecosystem make money in the first place, in order to achieve success in the long run.[23] If they are not connected to the right partners, it can be quite a challenge to get the required knowledge and experience level[24]. But there are more issues that need to be overcome. Organizations, ambitious as they may be, often work with outdated business models, and they are stuck in old habits. Not only do they need to engage new partners and experts, they also need to come up with a different strategy and a new architecture type in order to support all different kinds of IoT applications. Hence, every ISV starting with IoT will need the following sooner or later:

• A team of skilled and experienced specialists
• The right software architecture
• Insights into success factors that turn your IoT business into a source of revenue
• Insights into common pitfalls that may jeopardize your chances of success
• A business model defining the key elements of their strategy

Our success formula
There is only little information on IoT's economic and managerial background since it is a recent development, which makes it hard for ISVs to make informed decisions about adoption and implementation. That is why we challenged ourselves to come up with

22 Chan, H. (2015). **Internet of Things Business Models.** Journal of Service Science and Management, 8, 552-568.
23 Dijkman, R., Sprenkels, B., Peeters, T., & Janssen, A. (2015). **Business models for the Internet of Things.** International Journal of Information Management, 35, 672-678.
24 Andersson, P., & Mattsson, L. (2015). **Service innovations enabled by the "internet of things".** IMP Journal, 9 (1), 85-106.

some answers. We studied all of the requirements mentioned above in order to develop a success formula for ISVs preparing their business for IoT. What does their ultimate business model look like, how should they develop their software architecture, what challenges will they face and what competences do they need to overcome them? These were the things that crossed our minds, so we asked ourselves the following question, divided into four sub questions:

How can ISVs prepare for tomorrow's business in IoT?

What software architecture do they need as a basis?

Which challenges do they have to take into account?

Which competences are essential for their employees?

Which business model items are relevant?

We will get there (but not on this page)

You are probably impatient by now, and you want some answers. You will get them, but not right now. Before we provide all the answers, we will first explain the IoT concept, its key ingredients, and its main domains. You are going to need this information when selecting and applying the building blocks of your IoT business model. Just bear with us and we will get there, and you will not be sorry you spent some of your free time reading the following chapters, we promise!

6. ▸ Introducing the Internet of Things

The term "Internet of Things" is an umbrella keyword for all applications related to the extension of the internet and the web into the physical world. This extension is realized through spatially distributed devices with embedded identification, sensing and actuation capabilities.[25] In simpler words, IoT is a global network of machines and devices capable of interacting with each other through online applications. The interconnected objects in this network do not only collect information from their environment, they also use existing internet standards to provide services for information transfer, analytics, applications, and communication. You can find IoT applications in both the consumer market and in business applications, varying from a relatively simple connection between a smartphone and a thermostat to a global network of integrated systems that offer many services to their users combined. Think about automation and industrial manufacturing, logistics, business and process management, services, and intelligent transportation of people and goods.[26]

> **Fun fact.** The term "Internet of Things" was first documented by Kevin Ashton from the Massachusetts Institute of Technology in the year 1999[27]. At the time, the term was used to describe a networked system of autonomously interacting and self-organizing objects and processes. Not very different from today's interpretation of IoT, but incomparable in terms of usage!

In literature, interested readers will find two perspectives on IoT, which are a Things-oriented and an Internet-oriented perspective[28]. However, there is also a quite new, third perspective that is semantic-oriented, which is all about the knowledge that is derived from IoT information flows[29]. None of these perspectives

25 Miorandi, D., Sicari, S., De Pellegrini, F., & Chlamtac, I. (2012). **Internet of things: Vision, applications and research challenges.** Ad Hoc Networks, 10 (7), 1497–1516.
26 Atzori, L., Iera, A., & Morabito, G. (2010). **The Internet of Things: A survey.** Computer Networks.
27 Ashton, K. (2009). **That "Internet of Things" thing.** RFiD Journal.
28 Gubbi, J., Buyya, R., Marusic, S., & Palaniswami, M. (2013). **Internet of Things (IoT): A vision, architectural elements, and future directions.** Future Generation Computer Systems, 29, 1645-1660.
29 Atzori, L., Iera, A., & Morabito, G. (2010). **The Internet of Things: A survey.** Computer Networks.

or orientations is right or wrong, as IoT can have different end goals. The term is used for a wide array of applications, some of them resulting in devices working autonomously (Things-oriented), others integrating multiple systems (Internet-oriented), others gathering relevant data that can be interpreted to optimize performance and processes (Semantic-oriented). Hence, IoT offers value in three ways:

1. Through **middleware** (e.g. different corporate systems getting connected and integrated on a platform)
2. Through **things** (sensors enabling appliances to function autonomously)
3. Through **knowledge** (data getting analyzed and used for optimization of processes or performance)

In an ideal situation, you are able to offer value in all three ways at the same time, which is not unthinkable, as you can use the same application to control your devices, gather relevant data, integrate them with other data, and use the information to improve your products and services. This way, you optimally use the three main IoT components, which are the Internet, a Thing and Information flows. In the picture below, you see how they collaborate[4]:

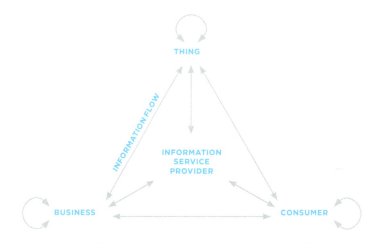

Information providers and information flows in IoT[4]

It is obvious that the Information Service Provider plays an essential role in this IoT triangle. It allows businesses to create services for their customers by getting them into contact with a 'thing', which can be pretty much everything, from a lamppost to an airplane. In most cases, IoT information flows come together on an online platform, where they are stored, integrated, and analyzed. This is what we call cloud computing. You will find more information on cloud computing in the next paragraph.

Main IoT ingredients

When starting with IoT, there are three ingredients that you should know about: IoT applications, middleware, and cloud computing. We will briefly discuss them in the upcoming sections.

IoT applications

First of all, let us zoom into IoT applications. Whereas networks only provide virtual connectivity, IoT applications enable device-to-device and human-to-device interactions. Not only do they exchange data, they also make things happen in the physical world[30]. IoT applications are the messenger that realizes a perfect integration between distributed systems and devices[29], and can be divided in three categories[27]: (1) web-based front-ends and portals, (2) dashboards, and (3) interactions with systems outside the network (so-called APIs). The last one is particularly important, as APIs enable information exchange beyond the boundaries of a corporate system or network, which means that they can integrate and connect pretty much everything.

"You would not learn to speak French fluently when all you need is a baguette, would you?"

Middleware

This is the software layer that enables software developers to connect IoT applications to one another[30]. This may sound complex, but the power of middleware lies in its simplicity; each and every single device, system, and software application has features and software services that are not directly relevant to the specific IoT application. Therefore, middleware only takes components that are needed for IoT integration, and hides all abundant

---

30 Lee, I., & Lee, K. (2015). **The Internet of Things (IoT): Applications, investments, and challenges for enterprises.** Business Horizons, 58, 431-440.

technologies. So instead of translating all languages into one common one, middleware only takes the words that are necessary for communication, just like you would do when you are in a foreign country. You would not learn to speak French fluently when all you need is a baguette, would you? Instead, you take what you need and find the right translation for it, so your message will come across and people get you the things you need. Middleware is just like that, but rather on a much larger scale. An IoT middleware architecture abstracts the devices, functionalities, and communication capabilities, providing a common set of services and an environment for service composition[26]. Being a translator, an integrator, and a manager in one, middleware should always be independent from devices and networks, with the purpose that it can be used to connect devices, systems, and software programs of any kind.

Cloud computing

Oh the cloud. It is the magic word of this era. But when talking about the cloud (sometimes even spelled with a capital letter to emphasize its importance), what do people actually mean? And even more important: do they even know what they mean? Simply put, the cloud is an online environment that allows us to simultaneously share, store, edit, and exchange information. Even though it is an online environment, this does not necessarily mean it is public. Organizations can choose to take their systems and processes to the cloud, but still keep them private. It provides them with an ideal back-end solution for handling huge data streams and processing them for the unprecedented number of IoT devices in real time. This makes IoT the biggest consumer of cloud computing[31].

Making sense of IoT domains

In the introduction, we discussed some examples of IoT domains, such as healthcare, education, and agriculture. Obviously, there are more. IoT appears in many forms and is not restricted to specific sectors. Making sense of all these examples and applications can be quite challenging, but it is essential if you want to get to know the concept you are dealing with. Accordingly, we will give you an overview of the existing domains in this chapter, so you get an idea of the scope of IoT.

---

31 Vermesan, O., Friess, P., Guillemin, P., Gusmeroli, S., Sundmaeker, H., Bassi, A., et al. (2009). **Internet of Things Strategic Research Roadmap.** Cluster of European Research Projects on the Internet of Things, CERP-IoT.

In literature, researchers distinguish three IoT domains[a]:

Domain	Description	Examples
Industry	Activities involving financial or commercial transactions between companies, organizations, and other entities.	Manufacturing, logistics, service sector, banking, financial governmental authorities, intermediaries, and so on.
Environment	Activities regarding the protection, monitoring, and development of all natural resources.	Agriculture and breeding, recycling, environmental management services, energy management, and so on.
Society	Activities / initiatives regarding the development and inclusion of society, cities, and people.	Governmental services towards citizens and other society structures (e-participation), e-inclusion (for disabled people and the elderly), and so on.

Regardless of the domain, IoT applications can be used for information and analysis (Internet-oriented and semantic-oriented), or automation and control (things-oriented), as you can see in the scheme below[a].

Domain	Type	Description
Information and analysis	Tracking behavior	Embedded products with sensors that track their movements and sometimes even monitor interactions with them.
	Enhanced situational awareness	Data from large numbers of sensors, deployed in an infrastructure (such as roads and buildings) that are used to report on environmental conditions (including soil moisture, ocean currents, the weather), so decision makers are well informed.
	Sensor-driven decision analytics	Support for longer-range, more complex planning and decision making.
Automation and control	Process optimization	Embedded sensors in the production process that track performances for optimization.
	Optimized resource consumption	Networked sensors and automated feedback mechanisms can change usage patterns for scarce resources, including energy and water, often by enabling more dynamic pricing.
	Complex autonomous systems	The most demanding use of IoT involves the rapid, real-time sensing of unpredictable conditions and instantaneous responses guided by automated systems. This kind of automated decision making mimics human reactions, determining its own follow up.

How to build your
IoT solution - by Paul Fremantle

7.

Paul Fremantle co-founded WSO2 after nine years at IBM, where he was a Senior Technical Staff Member. While at IBM, Paul created the Web Services Gateway, and led the team that developed and shipped it as part of the WebSphere Application Server. Paul has published many articles, two books, and is a frequent speaker at industry conferences. In 2016, he started his PHD at the University of Plymouth, where he studies security and scalability of the Internet of Things.

Now that you know all about IoT, you probably wonder who you are in this story. The truth is that you (being an ISV and all) will be playing a key role. As we explained in chapter 6, middleware is what connects the virtual world to the physical one, which means that without it, companies working with IoT will not get anywhere. Wherever there are cloud based medical records, smart fridges and internet connected cars, integration software is involved. This means that you will be the expert company creating the online environment where it all comes together. But how do you make it happen? How do you connect Things with the Internet and how do you get them to talk? And how do you turn data into useful information? Sadly, there is no clear answer to this question. There are helpful guidelines, though. In this chapter, we will talk you through something that is called the IoT reference architecture. A framework that will help you to establish everything you need to build your IoT solution. Afterwards, we will introduce you to the key of a successful IoT strategy: API management.

This chapter was based on two WSO2 white papers:

1: A Reference Architecture for the Internet of Things by Paul Fremantle[32]
2: API Management Platform Technical Evaluation Framework by Chris Haddad[33]

32 Fremantle, P. (2015). **A Reference Architecture for the Internet of Things.** WSO2.
33 Haddad, C. (2015). **API Management Platform Technical Evaluation Framework.** WSO2.

WSO2 is an international software company that offers middleware solutions to customers. Being 100% open source, cloud ready, and scalable, their enterprise platform is used by many preeminent companies all over the world. More information on WSO2 can be found on their corporate website: www.wso2.com.

"There is no roadmap and no step-to-step plan, because of the simple fact that companies working with IoT go where no one else has gone before"

Scalable and adaptable

Given that the IoT concept covers many different things, there are also many different network technologies involved, like sensors, beacons, Wi-Fi, connected phones, NFC, Bluetooth, and so on. Requirements differ per project, just like materials, the needed expertise, and other necessities. Your customers will come up with the most complex (but coolest) ideas, and they will turn to you for technical advice and implementation. Considering the many ideas that are out there, you will have no standard checklist that you can use for all of your IoT projects. There is no roadmap and no step-to-step plan, because of the simple fact that companies working with IoT go where no one else has gone before. So when you start with IoT, you should create an architecture that is both scalable and adaptable to all possible capabilities, requirements, and extras, which are needed to turn crazy ideas into reality. Therefore, WSO2 introduced the IoT reference architectur: a vendor neutral framework that you can use to establish every single process, system, device, and means of communication you may need. So no matter who comes knocking on your door: you will have everything it takes to get this customer's IoT project started and make all of his wishes come true.

Reference Architecture Elements

So when you start with IoT, what do you need from a technological point of view? In the infographic below you will see the different layers of the IoT reference architecture. First of all, you need a place, a platform if you will, where you can collect your data before they are sent to the next layer to be analyzed and processed. This part is called Aggregation/Bus Layer, ESB, and Message Broker. Simply put, this is the place where all messages come together to get sorted. The data is derived from devices (cellphones; cows; thermostats; cars) and is connected to the bus layer through communication protocols, such as HTTP or MQTT. This process is managed by a Devices Manager, that controls the connected devices and remotely manages the deployed software and applications. As soon as the data is sorted in the bus layer, it is shipped to the Event Processing and Analytics Layer, where the messages are analyzed and turned into actions. The top layer consists of a Web Portal, a Dashboard, and API Management and together they enable external (or client) communication. All of the above should be closely monitored through your Identity & Access Management, which means that the right people and data streams have access to the right systems of the different layers. ...Are you still there?

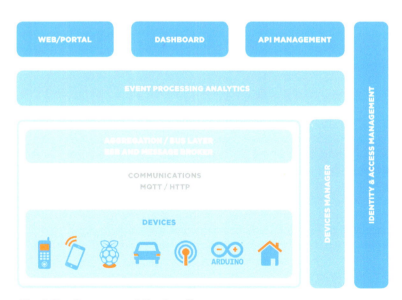

The IoT reference architecture[32]

" You should find clever ways to update, manage, and monitor all of the IoT devices, even if they were never designed to interact"

Requirements

Implementing all of the elements above is a great way to start, but it will not get you very far if you do not comply with some specific requirements. IoT devices interact non-stop, which means that you should come up with a high availability solution. This also means that you need to find ways to perform disaster recovery without taking down the system. Moreover, you should find clever ways to update, manage, and monitor all of the IoT devices, even if they were never designed to interact. This is what the API (Application Programming Interface) is for. APIs are an essential component of your IoT reference architecture, as they form the bridge between you and the outside world. Just

installing them will not do the trick, though. APIs need to be taught how to communicate, and most important of all, they need to be managed. We could write ten books on API management and we still would not have covered the entire subject, so on the next page, you will find a short introduction to get you started.

It is up to you

So there you have it: the IoT reference architecture in a nutshell. The combination of features and layers mentioned above forms the basis of any IoT project, meaning your company will be of inestimable value to your customers that want to start one. As an integration expert, it is your job to make all the layers work together and optimize the data streams. Sure, the customer will take the credits for the idea, and he will be the owner of the data, but without you, he would have ended up with nothing but a Thing and the Internet. You, on the other hand, know how to connect devices with bus layers and portals, integrate data, and to monitor, update, and secure the entire process. In other words, if you want to be able to provide each customer with a suited IoT solution, you should make sure you know how to integrate all the different layers, so everything is connected and runs smoothly. If you get it right, you will become a crucial partner whom your customers cannot operate without. And why would they even want to, when you bring so much to the table?

"Uber has turned something simple like a taxi service into a concept that supports customers in their daily life"

The brilliance of APIs

The fun thing about APIs is the fact that they allow you to combine, mix, and use data and functionalities from everywhere, both online and offline. An API is like an intelligent revolving door, structuring and analyzing data streams before they are sent off to their next stop. In contrast to other IoT applications, such as web based front-ends, APIs are able to connect to pretty much everything, whether it is a CMS or a windmill. Another great thing about APIs is that you can make them public so external developers can join in. This results in a wealth of new opportunities and applications. Let us illustrate this by telling you about one of our favorite API examples: Uber.

Case study: Uber

Uber started working with APIs and has done amazing things. The American multinational offers taxi rides which can be booked through an API that is connected to a smartphone app. This way, payments can be done more safely and customers are instantly informed about times of arrival. What is even more interesting, is that Uber has opened up their app to external developers, and thus they have created a platform in which their taxi services have been integrated with other apps and services. Up until now, they have integrated Uber with an app for the Windows Phone, smartwatch Pebble, transport app Transit, OpenTable (an application consumers use to discover and book restaurants), and airline company United, to name a few. In other words, Uber has turned something simple like a taxi service into a concept that supports customers in their daily life, by taking care of their transportation needs and their quest for the hotspots in every city. This is what APIs can do.

Resource accessibility

As the Uber app shows, APIs integrate different services by combining different data systems of different applications. This is good news, not least for companies with a complex infrastructure of data systems that do not know how to communicate. Most systems have their own coding language, and are consequently incompatible with other systems, even within companies. By bringing together different systems through an API, for example systems for monetization, product support and HR, you can create a silo for all your data. This way you receive more in-sights into revenue streams, staff turnover, key resources, and customer segments, since you have access to the same database for different purposes and analyses.

The brilliance of API Management

All of this integrating, connecting, and communicating comes with a price. If not well managed, security and privacy are at stake, creating serious problems for both systems and people. Therefore, it is key that data gets encrypted, regularly updated, and monitored by the best API manager you can find. APIs may seem like brilliance that lights itself, they still need to be managed. So whether you provide an open API to the public or a (paid) closed API to your specific business partner, as a provider you should look for a suitable platform to get access to your API, in order to have it set up, protected, and optimized. This means that you will need a solution for access management, SLA policies, Quality of Service, and API Throttling policies. And of course you need a store where all your APIs can be explored by the end-consumer. Such a solution is called an API Manager, and it is what gets your API to work. A solid API manager is a complete solution for designing and publishing APIs, creating and managing a developer community, while facilitating scalable routing API traffic. It also integrates and governs all software components and offers a Data Analytics Server for analytics, which gives you instant insight into API behavior. You are going to need all of this to get the best out of your API. The last thing you want is external parties taking down your infrastructure or stealing your data.

▸ IoT pitfalls

Despite our enthusiasm for the subject, we cannot deny that innovation comes with challenges. Especially in the online world, where our data is often out of sight and shared with many people we will never meet in real life, we have to be careful. Plus, when starting something new, you are going to run into some teething problems eventually. The best thing for you to do, is make sure you are aware of the risks and challenges so you can anticipate and solve them before they escalate. In the case of IoT, researchers often report on problems such as security and privacy, which means that you should build security and privacy into your devices, rather than adding them later on in the process[34]. Technology can be tricky as well, especially when you are no techie yourself or when your team members lack technological skills. Those obstacles are not invincible, but some inside information will come in handy. In this chapter, we will look into the main IoT challenges based on the findings of our literature study.

"Confidence in and acceptance of IoT will mostly depend on the protection of users' privacy"

Privacy

When it comes to privacy, the biggest issue is authorization and access control for data produced and consumed by IoT applications[35]. Take smart health equipment and smart car emergency services for example. IoT applications are able to collect a vast amount of data on IoT users' location and movements, health conditions, and purchasing preferences, which can spark significant privacy concerns[30]. Protecting the privacy of IoT users is

---

34 Waltzman, H., & Shen, L. (2015). **The Internet of Things.** Intellectual Property & Technology Law Journal, 27 (7), 19-21.

35 Fremantle, P., Aziz, B., Kopecký, J., & Scott, P. (2014). **Federated Identity and Access Management for the Internet of Things.** 3rd International Workshop on the Secure IoT (pp. 10-17). Wroclaw: IEEE.

counterproductive for service providers in this scenario, as data generated by IoT is key to improving the quality of people's lives and decreasing service providers' costs by streamlining opera-tions[30]. Organizations need to combine the data they gathered from IoT applications with other information, in order to make as-sumptions about consumer behavior and adapt their services and products in a meaningful way[34]. However, while IoT continues to gain momentum through smart home systems and wearable de-vices, confidence in and acceptance of IoT will mostly depend on the protection of users' privacy[33]. In case you are wondering how you can fully protect the privacy of your users, read the "Bill of Rights" by Limor Fried[36]; a statement piece that campaigns for transparent and open IoT applications. Key motivators are[36]:

- Always prefer open over closed, so portability
  between IoT devices is ensured.
- Consumers, not companies, should own the data collected
  by IoT devices.
- IoT devices that collect public data must reveal these data.
- Consumers have the right to keep their data private.
- Consumers have the right to delete or back up data
  collected by IoT devices.

Use these statements as your guiding principles for IoT service providers, and you are well on your way to respecting your us-ers' privacy. In 2015, the U.S. Federal Trade Commission (FTC) re-leased a report titled "Internet of Things – Privacy and Security in a Connected World", highlighting the issues involved with IoT, and detailing the steps that organizations can take to enhance and protect their users' privacy. Although the FTC's recommendations are not mandatory, you should take advantage of their guidelines, as they might become mandatory in the future and you should make sure you are on top of your game when it comes to protect-ing your users' privacy[34]. It is better to prevent beforehand than to cure afterwards when it comes to trust and support. One last tip: never think you have everything covered. New privacy issues will arise as technology evolves, and people with bad intentions will always find new ways of sabotaging your systems. If you are not sure whether your IoT applications are safe, contact someone who can help you.

36 Fried, L. (2014, May 15). **A Bill of Rights for the Internet of Things.** Retrieved January 30, 2016, from The New York Times: http://www.nytimes.com/roomfordebate/2013/09/08/privacy-and-the-internet-of-things/a-bill-of-rights-for-the-internet-of-things

"IoT devices are not just vulnerable because of the lack of transport encryption, but their web interfaces are often poorly protected, software protection is inadequate, and authorization is insufficient"

Security

Although the importance of security is widely known among business owners and IT developers, IoT brings new security challenges to the table[37]. The number and variety of devices that are connected to an IoT network increases, and consequently the security threats will increase too. Traditional security countermeasures cannot be directly applied to IoT technologies due to the different standards and communication stacks involved[38]. IoT may improve the productivity of organizations and the quality of people's lives, it will also increase the potential attack surfaces for hackers and other cyber criminals[30]. These include network threats as well as physical threats to devices. Due to the inexpensive hardware and low-power, IoT devices are often not suitable for high-strength encryption and signature algorithms, which makes them vulnerable against attacks[35]. Apart from the encryption problem, the volume of IoT connected devices may cause serious security management issues[37]. IoT devices are not just vulnerable because of the lack of transport encryption, but their web interfaces are often poorly protected, software protection is inadequate, and authorization is insufficient[39].

Privacy and security overlap in a way that a lack of security will create resistance to adopting IoT by both organizations and consumers[30]. Thus if you want your IoT applications to become a

[37] Mathon, J. (2015, September 8). **Security and Privacy – Not the staid and boring business of the past 20 years.** Retrieved February 6, 2016, from CloudRamblings: http://cloudramblings. me/2015/09/08/security-and-privacy-not-the-staid-and-boring-business-of-the-past-20-years/

[38] Sicari, S., Rizzardi, A., Grieco, L., & Coen-Porisini, A. (2015). **Security, privacy and trust in Internet of Things:** The road ahead. Computer Networks (76), 146–164.

[39] Hewlett Packard. (2014, July 29). **HP Study Reveals 70 Percent of Internet of Things Devices Vulnerable to Attack.** Retrieved February 6, 2016, van http://www8.hp.com/us/en/hp-news/press-release.html?id=1744676#.VrZNR4-cFR0

success, you cannot go without a valid security model for the IoT application context. It is simply the only way to get your customers on board[40]. This means that data anonymity, confidentiality, integrity, and authentication and authorization mechanisms that prevent unauthorized users to get access to your systems, need to be guaranteed[38].

"Today, there are well over a dozen different protocols and standards for internet-connected devices"

Technological issues

Privacy and security are one thing, but technology itself is quite another. The first stage of the IoT development was characterized by the appearance of many different protocols, which resulted in individual solutions that were completely non-compatible with each other, as is often the case with new network technologies[41]. Due to this diversity in protocols, there is no common way of connecting one device or system to another, which means that the task of finding a device must be reduced to finding a web-service representing the device in the network. These services either operate on devices themselves or run on special middleware data platforms. Thus each single device should get its virtual online representation in order to work on a global scale, and therefore a search schema has to be standardized so that it is capable to integrate device information[41]. However, this problem can be solved by using an API which integrates systems that would seem incompatible at first sight. For example, you could use an API to connect your fridge to your smartphone, even though your fridge has never been taught how to talk to telephones.

Today, there are well over a dozen different protocols and standards for internet-connected devices. John Mathon foresees that this number will decline as the market converges, but the different requirements for communication are real and will require different solutions, which means that there will never be a single IoT

---

40 Weber, R. (2010). **Internet of Things – New security and privacy challenges.** Internet of Things – New security and privacy challenges, 26 (1), 23-30.

41 Efremov, S., Pilipenko, N., & Voskov, L. (2015). **An Integrated Approach to Common Problems in the Internet of Things.** 25th DAAAM International Symposium on Intelligent.

protocol or communication paradigm[42]. For example, some devices have persistent always-on communication, whereas many other devices cannot afford that level of connectivity. Basically, there are three models of device-to-device communication, which are:

• Direct access
• Communication through a gateway
• Middleware data platforms

In the case of direct access, one of the interacting devices acts as a web-server and requires high processing capabilities, which cannot be implemented on every device. It is a complicated task for embedded systems to provide direct network access, and since many technologies focus on maximizing energy-efficiency, their processing capabilities are very limited, which makes it pretty much impossible to implement a complete network stack on a microcontroller[41]. The problem can be solved by using a gateway, which uses HTTP for communication and supports specialized protocols for devices interaction[41]. The gateway acts as a web-server, while a middleware data platform provides a centralized point to store, search, control, and visualize data from IoT devices. Thanks to this solution, different information systems can be built on top of middleware platforms, which is exactly what Dutch multinational Philips did when they launched Philips Healthsuite, an online platform that integrates patient data and device information. Data that has been derived from systems, devices, and people are brought together on a middleware data platform that turns these data into useful information for doctors and patients themselves[43].

42 Mathon, J. (2015, Juni 22). **What is the difference between Services, Device, Apps, APIs and Microservices.** Retrieved April 30, 2016, from CloudRamblings: https://cloudramblings.me/2015/06/22/services-micro-services-devices-apps-apis-whats-the-difference/
43 More information: http://www.philips.nl/healthcare/innovatie/healthsuite-digital-platform

▶ Success factor 1. Competences

9.

Having read about the obstacles and challenges that come with IoT, you might wonder what it is you need to succeed. As we told you in the introduction, most of it boils down to a solid business model. That is not enough though. Companies that disrupted their sector with IoT all possessed comparable core competences that seem to be indispensable for rising to great heights. Your plan may be brilliant, but if the executors lack courage, strong analytical skills, and a long term focus, it will not get you very far. In the specific case of IoT, you will need a combination of management capabilities and difficult-to-imitate organizational, functional, and technological skills[44]. Without them, you will not be able to analyze sources and methods of wealth creation that organizations, which operate in environments of rapid technological change such as ISVs, desperately need. An ISV needs to master multiple disciplines, such as the ability to oversee and connect processes within their client's departments and their value chain in order to be a good interlocutor[45]. In literature, researchers agree on the fact that organizations which undergo major technological changes should have the right mix of knowledge, skills, and abilities[46] [47]. In the schedule you can see what they came up with.

> "In the specific case of IoT, you will need a combination of management capabilities and difficult-to-imitate organizational, functional, and technological skills"

[44] Teece, D. (2010). **Business model, business strategy and innovation.** Long Range Plan, 43 (2-3), 172-194.

[45] ABN AMRO. (2016). **Industrial Internet of Things: Noodzaak voor Industrie, kans voor IT-sector.**

[46] Rouw, A. (2016). **Human Resource Practices to Prepare for Robots in the Corporate World.** Breukelen: Nyenrode Business Universiteit.

[47] Renck, R., Kahn, E., & Gardner, B. (1969). **Continuing Education in R&D Careers.** DSF Report 69-20, Prepared by the Social Research, Inc.

Take your time to read this thoroughly. Which competences does your organization already have, and which ones are a work in progress? This might be the moment to evaluate internal problems which could lead to trouble in the future. Better safe than sorry!

Competence	Explanation
Social intelligence	The capability to manage complicated social connections and situations
Creativity	The production of something original and worthwhile
Problem solving skills	Working through the components of a problem in order to find the solution
Cognition	Judging, knowing, learning, perceiving, recognizing, remembering, thinking, and understanding that lead to the awareness of the world around us
Flexibility	The ability to change when the situation requires it
Critical thinking	Examining and reconsidering assumptions in order to find the hidden values, and evaluate the evidence and conclusions that are presented
Analytic skills	Studying past historical data to research potential trends, to analyze the effects of certain decisions or events, or to evaluate the performance of a given tool or scenario.
Technical skills	The knowledge and abilities needed to accomplish mathematical, engineering, scientific, or computer-related duties, as well as other specific tasks.

Success factor 2. Business models

10

Let us say you took some time to solve all your internal issues and worked on the technical skills of your colleagues or fellow employees. You brought in some creative thinkers to complete your project team and you are pretty sure you are ready to start with IoT. What do you do next? That is right, you develop a strategy. The best way to do this, is by developing your own business model. Organizations use business models to bring technological innovations to the market, and thus these are key to determining failure or success. Organizations that brought disruptive change to their industry, innovated on their business model rather than on technical details. An example is the rise of the low-cost airlines, which represented a significant innovation in transportation, though the major change they introduced was based on a shift in their business model and not on any technical aspects of the flight. This also applies to Tesla, which is not the fastest car in the industry, and it does not have the strongest engine. It is the cleverest car, though, and it offers services that other car manufacturers would have never thought of in the first place.

"Organizations that brought disruptive change to their industry, innovated on their business model rather than on technical details"

Key elements

Business models revolve around the key elements that cover the strategic choices that businesses deal with, the resources that enable them to create value, their position in their value network, and a high-level definition of their cost and revenue structures. Once a business model has been developed, it is possible to develop a matching strategy, business plans, and to forecast future financial outcomes. Therefore, an organization's business model is the starting point from which the organization can develop all its future actions. It provides a high-level description of "what" the organization will do, while the aim of the business strategy is rather to state "how" this can be effectively achieved.

"A successful IoT business model simply cannot be a classical one, as it should be disruptive, original, and hard to copy"

No bakery

A baker's business model is relatively simple: he buys ingredients such as flour, eggs, and sugar, and turns these ingredients into bread and pastries which he sells at the counter. If the baker is lucky, people will like his products and they will buy them on a regular basis, so that the baker makes enough money to pay the salaries of his employees, and to buy more ingredients and bakery supplies, which help him to produce more bread and pastries. In the case of ISVs, this process is slightly more complicated, as they do not sell bread, or any other tangible product. ISVs offer services that help organizations to integrate their corporate systems, databases, and information flows, and to optimize their services towards clients. Even though the current business model for ISVs works perfectly fine, ISVs starting with IoT do not survive on the common, classical business formats they used to work with[48]. A successful IoT business model simply cannot be a classical one, as it should be disruptive, original, and hard to copy. Hence, developing an IoT business model is a challenge on its own.

Which one?!

So you need a business model, but which one? That is what we have been asking ourselves as well. That is why we dove into a pile of studies conducted by both European and American researchers and found a lot of information on business models. Like most researchers, none of them agreed on which business model was the right one, and many of them developed their own. Most of these models, however, revolve around the four questions Who, What, How, and Why[49]. "Who" refers to the target customer, "What" is the value proposition that is offered to the customer, "How" is the value chain driver to deliver the value proposition to the customer,

48 Mahadevan, B. (2000). **Business models for Internet-based e-commerce: An anatomy.** California management review, 42 (4), 55-69.
49 Gassmann, O., Frankenberger, K., & Csik, M. (2014). **Revolutionizing the business model.** In Management of the Fuzzy Front End of Innovation (pp. 89-97). Springer International Publishing.

and "Why" describes the underlying economic model to capture value. The interconnection between these four essential elements is depicted in the figure below:

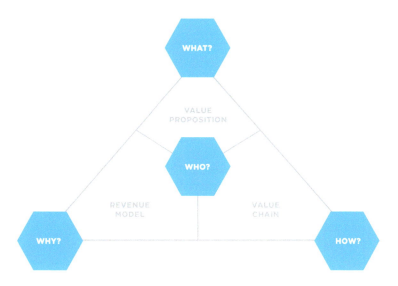

The archetypal business model[51]

Business Model Canvas

We found many other business models that were all based on this Who, What, How, and Why-model. After a thorough literature review and extensive comparisons, we came to the conclusion that most researchers studying IoT and IoT business models used the Business Model Canvas. This framework consists of nine building blocks that together outline the way organizations intend to make money. The building blocks cover four main areas of a business, which are customers, proposition, infrastructure, and financial viability. The Business Model Canvas (BMC) can be used as a strategy blueprint to implement business structures, processes, and systems. Let us have a look at the schedule on the next page.

50 Osterwalder, A., & Pigneur, Y. (2002). **An e-business model ontology for modeling e-business.** 15th Bled Electronic Commerce Conference.
51 Gassmann, O., Frankenberger, K., & Csik, M. (2014). **The Business Model Navigator.** Harlow: Pearson.

Business Model Canvas[50]

Key Partners	Key Activities	Value Propositions	Customer Relationships	Customer Segments
	Key Resources		Channels	
Cost Structure			Revenue Streams	

The BMC describes a business by dividing its features into nine building blocks. Read the list below and think about the way your organization has been doing business the last couple of years. Do not skip one single business block; together the nine items form a whole.

1. **Customer Segments:** the different groups of people or organizations an organization aims to reach and serve.
2. **Value propositions:** the bundle of products and services that create value for a specific customer segment.
3. **Channels:** modes of communication an organization uses to reach its customer segments.
4. **Customer Relationships:** the types of relationships an organization maintains with specific customer segments.
5. **Revenue Streams:** the ways an organization generates cash from the customer segments they serve.
6. **Key Resources:** the most important resources required to create and offer a value proposition.
7. **Key Activities:** the most important actions an organization undertakes to create and offer value.
8. **Key Partners:** the network of suppliers and partners an organization needs to create and offer value.
9. **Cost Structure:** the different costs an organization makes to create and offer value.

Each of the building blocks consists of several building block items, that were based on previous studies using the Business Model Canvas. The model is a starting-point rather than a static format, meaning you can leave out the items that do not apply to your organization and add the ones that do. By doing this, you create your very own business model. In the figure below, you will see what we will call the Standard Business Model Canvas for IoT applications. Hence the model as we found it in literature studies.

"Middleware is what connects the virtual world to the physical one, which means that without it, companies working with IoT will not get anywhere"

Standard Business Model Canvas[50]

Key Partners	Key Activities	Value Propositions	Customer Relationships	Customer Segments
Software developers	Product development	Convenience/ usability	Communities	Multi-side platforms
Launching customers	Software development	"Getting the job done"	Co-creation	Mass market
Data interpretation	Customer development	Performance	Self-service	Diversified
Hardware producers	Service; implementation	Possibility for updates	Automated service	Niche market
Service partners Distributors	Platform development	Comfort	Personal assistance	Segmented
Other suppliers	Sales; marketing	Accessibility	Dedicated assistance	
Logistics	Partner management Logistics	Cost reduction		

	Key Resources	Risk reduction	**Channels**	
	Software	Customization	Web sales	
	Employee capabilities	Design	Partner stores	
	Relations	Price	Sales force	
	Physical resources	Newness	Wholesaler	
	Intellectual property	Brand/status	Own stores	
	Financial resources			

Cost Structure	**Revenue Streams**
Product development cost	Subscription fees
IT cost	Usage fee
Hardware/production cost	Asset sale
Personnel cost	Lending/renting/leasing
Marketing & sales cost	Licensing
Logistics cost	Advertising
	Startup fees
	Installation fees
	Brokerage fees

Business model archetypes

When working with IoT, your success will not be based on innovative products and processes, but on innovative business models[51]. You need that something special that sets you apart from your competition and makes you exceed the expectations of your customers. Therefore, it is key that you select a model that does just that. The best way to start, is by looking at some examples that have proven their success in the past. Take the "low-cost carrier model" by EasyJet, or the full service providers like Tesla and smart thermostat developers. These so called business model archetypes can be found all over the world, in every single segment you can think of. You are probably busy, so we are not going to bore you by naming them all. Instead, we have selected six business model archetypes that are specifically useful to IT organizations. These are:

• Freemium
• Leverage customer data
• Open source
• Pay per use
• Subscription
• Two-sided market

Freemium

The word 'freemium' is a combination of 'free' and 'premium' and offers both a basic version of a product or service that is free of charge, and a premium version against additional payment. The free version of the product or service is used to get customers on the right track, so they will hopefully see the value of the more elaborate and expensive product and take the plunge and get the premium version[51]. The first freemium business models were web-based email services developed in the 1990s, such as Microsoft's Hotmail. Other well-known freemium-based businesses are Dropbox and LinkedIn. The success factor of this freemium pattern lies in the low operational costs (close to zero!) and the benefit of external network effects.

Leverage customer data

Customers leave digital traces all over the internet, which are highly relevant to organizations trying to get a grip on their target groups. These data are so called Big Data and form the main ingredients of the leverage customer data business model[51]. Amazon and Google are well on their way to becoming the world's largest data supermarket, by analyzing the interests and behavior of their users and selling it to those interested. To capitalize on the collected data, Amazon uses sales data to determine the relationships between different products and finds out which purchases result in follow-up acquisitions, and thus stimulating customers to buy additional goods. Google generates ninety percent of its revenue through advertising with its AdWords service, acquiring data through a myriad of free services such as search engines, personal calendars, email accounts, maps, and rating systems. Facebook and Twitter also rely strongly on this business model archetype.

Open source

Open source products are developed by a public community rather than a single organization. The source code is publicly accessible so that anyone can join in and contribute in his or her own way. As a result, the solutions developed do no longer belong to one organization in particular, but to the public as a whole. Since no income can be generated with the developed products, indirect returns get generated through products and services that build on an open source foundation. Organizations that use this business model do not have to invest in the development of new products. Despite its public character and bottom up approach, open source has proven that it can be enterprise grade. WSO2, for example, allows organizations to make billions of transactions a day using its software, and today even the most preeminent organizations in the world use open source all over their enterprise infrastructure[52]. Open source has found wide application in software design[51]. The connection of thousands of new services in the cloud will spur a technological and disruptive value in the effect of combining and using combinations of these services. Today's greatest example of an organization that created such a disruptive value is probably taxi firm Uber[53].

Pay per use

In the pay per use model, the specific usage of a service or product by the customer is metered and charged[51]. The price may be based on the number of units used, the volume that was consumed, or the duration of the usage. A considerable advantage for customers is that the costs are highly transparent. The pay per use pattern also spurred the creation of a variety of innovative business models including the internet advertising "pay per click" model[49]. IoT is speeding up the shift towards this business model archetype, as both are focused on usage instead of ownership[45]. The pay per use pattern derives its enormous potential from this new product-founded ability to gather and analyze information[51]. For example, the organization Vanderlande, a Dutch organization for luggage handling in airports, offers its services for a fixed price

[52] Mathon, J. (2013, November 8). **Inner Source, Open source for the enterprise.** Retrieved April 26, 2016, from CloudRamblings: https://cloudramblings.me/2013/11/08/inner-source-open-source-for-the-enterprise/

[53] Mathon, J. (2014, July 26). **The technology "disruption" occurring in today's business world is driven by open source and APIs and a new paradigm of enterprise collaboration.** Retrieved April 26, 2016, from CloudRamblings: https://cloudramblings.me/2014/07/26/the-technology-disruption-occurring-in-todays-business-world-is-driven-by-open-source-and-apis-and-a-new-paradigm-of-enterprise-collaboration/

per suitcase instead of selling the luggage handling system to the customer[45].

Subscription

Subscription allows customers to receive products or services regularly. This business model archetype revolves around a contract between a company and its customers, defining the frequency and length of the provision of services or products. Customers either pay for the services in advance or at regular intervals[49]. They often get a discount, as their subscription reassures the organization of a constant revenue stream. In order for subscriptions to work in the long term, it is important that customers perceive the benefits of the system and never feel that they have been tricked[49]. An example of this business model archetype is the cloud computing company Salesforce, whose customer relationship management (CRM) software is available as a series of products within a centralized cloud. Customers of Salesforce pay a monthly fee to access the company's software and all updates online. Another example is the Dutch software company Twinfield, which offers an online accounting platform with a proposition quite similar to the one by Salesforce. The subscription business model archetype is ideal when customers need the product or service on a regular basis. However, a subscription should always provide customers with additional value in order to be viable, such as less time required to purchase products or services, continued availability or less risk[49].

Two-sided market

The two-sided market business model archetype is a platform concept where two groups collaborate for mutual benefit. Central to this platform concept are so-called indirect network effects: the more customers use the platform, the more attractive it becomes to other customers. The main challenge in operating through such a platform is to steer the two customer groups in such a way that the network effects get maximized[49]. In order for a two-sided market to work, first the chicken or the egg problem needs to be resolved; as long as there are no customers using the platform, there is no incentive for others to join it. The situation thus calls for a speedy visibility of the platform by means of far-reaching ad campaigns and special offers[54]. A great example of a two-sided

---

54 Lin, M., Li, S., & Whinston, A. (2011). **Innovation and price competition in a two-sided market.** Journal of Information Systems Management, 28 (2), 171-202.

market is the ad-funded business model run by JCDecaux, which connects advertisers to consumers through indirect network effects. Other upcoming two-sided markets are the IoT platforms by Microsoft and Google, respectively Microsoft Azure IoT Suite and Google Eddystone for Beacons. A multi-sided business model that connects various parties is a must for all modern organizations, as traditional one-on-one models no longer suffice to compete in the market successfully. Understanding relevant stakeholders and how they are connected is of great importance, though[51].

Ok, so much for the business model archetypes. Time to find out what it all means in real life. Let's hear from some experts!

11. ▸Who were the experts?

When starting something new, it is always a good idea to ask around and hear stories from experience experts. What obstacles did they overcome, which tools did they use, who did they turn to for help? Especially in the case of IoT, preparation is key and expert stories might just make the difference between success and failure. This is the reason why we set out to find as many views on IoT applications as we possibly could. Luckily, at Yenlo, we do not lack driven business consultants, innovation evangelists, enterprise architects, solution architects, IoT developers, CEOs with a vision, and employees in sales and marketing. We selected ten of them, a group consisting of IoT experts exclusively. From now on, let us call them the Yenlo gurus. Apart from their stories, we also wanted to hear from experts outside the four walls of our company. Being an ISV, we are indeed involved in many IoT projects, but we do not have to deal with end customers, direction boards, and other B2C related issues. Therefore, we selected sixteen IoT experts who work in different sectors and who work on different IoT projects, resulting in a composition of visionaries, practitioners, and business partners with mixed IoT experiences and visions. They were all selected based on their affinity with IT, innovation, and IoT, and -obviously- their willingness to participate in the study. From this page on, we call them the external experts.

The interviews

We could have sent our experts an e-mail, asking for their view on IoT and the perfect IoT business model. Obviously, we did not. If you want answers, you have to talk to people in person. So instead of sending all those emails, we sat down with each one of the experts and listened to what they had to say. Each conversation would take around 70 minutes, meaning there was plenty of time to unravel the mysteries of the IoT world. We prepared a fixed set of questions, based on the Business Model Canvas and let our experts do the talking. Basically, what we did was tackling all the building blocks of the Canvas model, to see which blocks were said to be important, why, and in what way they should be put to use. This way, we collected all the puzzle pieces we needed to gain in-depth knowledge on IoT, essential competences to develop and exploit IoT applications, and insight in IoT barriers.

"Especially in
the case of IoT,
preparation is key
and expert stories
might just make the
difference between
success and failure"

Expert details

So who exactly were these Yenlo gurus and external experts? Let us take a look at some sample details. Due to privacy reasons, we chose to leave out the names of the interviewees.

External experts

Industry type

Industry	Number of interviewees
Advertisement	1x
Consultancy	1x
Education	1x
Energy	1x
Healthcare	2x
IT Hardware	1x
Public	3x
Retail	1x
Security	1x
Software	3x
Transportation	1x

Company size, client focus and type of offer

Size	Number of interviewees
Micro (<10 employees)	2x
Small (10-50 employees)	2x
Medium (50-250 employees)	3x
Large (>250 employees)	9x

Clients	
B2B	10
B2C	6

Product or service	
Product	4
Service	6
Both	6

Yenlo gurus

Industry type

Industry	Number of interviewees
IT Software (Yenlo)	10x

 *yeah duh...*

Job role, experience level

Job role	Number of interviewees
Founder	2
Evangelist / Trainer WSO2	1
Solution Architect	5
Delivery Manager Benelux	1
Pre-sales consultant	1

Years of experience in IoT	
<3 years	7
3 years	3

Fine-tuning the Business Model Canvas

When you look at the Business Model Canvas, you will see that there are nine building blocks (such as Key Partners, Revenue Streams, and Customer Relationships). Each of those building blocks contains a list of building block elements. The block Key Partners, for example, consists of Software developers, Launching customers, Hardware producers, and so on. However, the Business Model Canvas was never created to gain insights into ISV's working with IoT in particular, meaning it might contain elements that do not apply to your situation, and it could miss important elements that do. So, in order to fine-tune the Business Model Canvas to our field of research, we have only incorporated the elements that were mentioned by at least 25% of our external experts or internal IoT gurus. In other words, when an element (whether incorporated in the Standard Business Model Canvas or not) was discussed by seven or more interviewees, it would make it to the next round, whereas elements that were only mentioned once or twice were brutally eliminated, resulting in a business model framework focused on ISVs working with IoT. We made two brand new versions, the first one based on the interviews with the external experts, the second one based on the input of our IoT gurus. In these new versions, which we will both discuss in the upcoming chapters, the new elements are in **bold**. As you might have noticed, this is where it gets -very- interesting.

Key elements for a business in IoT – according to the external experts

Below, you see the Revised Business Model Canvas according to the external experts. As you can see, a few things have changed in comparison with the Standard Business Model Canvas. Some elements were not deemed important or relevant by the external experts (e.g. stores, software resources,
logistics) and were thus left out, whereas others were added to the model (e.g. research and development, security, freemium).
What building block items did the external experts mention, and what were their experiences? Let us hear it from them personally.

Revised Business Model Canvas according to the external experts

Key Partners	Key Activities	Value Propositions	Customer Relationships	Customer Segments
Software developers	Platform development	Convenience/ usability	Co-creation	Mass market
Launching customers	Partner management	Comfort	Communities	Niche market
Hardware producers	Research and development	Accessibility	Personal assistance	Segmented
Service partners	Software development	Services Domain expertise		
Network providers	Sales; marketing	Possibility for updates		
	Information architecture	Security		
	Service; implementation	Cost reduction		
		Customization		
	Key Resources	Design	**Channels**	
	Employee capabilities	Performance	Web sales	
	Financial resources	Newness		
	Physical resources			

Cost Structure	Revenue Streams
Product development cost	Usage fee
IT cost	Subscription fees
Hardware/production cost	Prototyping/pilots
Personnel cost	Two-sides market
Standardization cost	Leverage customer data
Service cost	Asset sale
	Adoption
	Freemium

Building block 1. Customer Segments

"All large organizations focus on large market shares, but you can earn quite some money in a niche"

The first building block of the Business Model Canvas consists of three forms of customer segments, which are niche market, mass market, and segmented. Twenty-five percent of the experts state you should focus on mainstream consumer goods, since this is where the IoT applications are most wanted. A second group of experts claims IoT should be implemented in different customer segments, since its many possibilities make it an ideal tool to target several market segments at once. However, a broad majority of the external experts (nearly 50%) believe in the power of small, as being disruptive means you should get off the highway and go to places that heavyweights cannot reach. If you go where the others cannot go, there is no competition to beat.

Themes	Percentage of responses	Quote
Niche market	47%	"...you have to be in a small back corner of the market, a niche, that is not interesting for others. All large organizations focus on large market shares, but you can earn quite some money in a niche. You will not find large organizations there, simply because it is not interesting enough for them." (interviewee 8)
Mass market	27%	"...the target audience for IoT can be found in consumer goods..." (interviewee 4)
Segmented	27%	"When looking at the electoral list of the water board elections, we have several target groups. By using IoT we are able to serve these target groups in a segmented way." (interviewee 14)

Building block 2. Value Propositions

"Companies should use data not only to provide you with better services, but also to optimize their products through constant updates"

When it comes to the actual value of the IoT offerings, usability is an absolute favorite among the external experts. IoT is meant to make lives easier, so that is exactly what your company should aim for. Consequently, it is no surprise that usability, comfort, and accessibility are highly valued by our interviewees. Even services, mentioned by 60% of the experts, should revolve around the customer.

Themes	Percentage of responses	Example quote
Convenience/ usability	80%	*"The usability factor of IoT devices and their quality are absolutely key, because they have an impact on real life." (interviewee 12)*
Comfort	67%	*"Companies should use data not only to provide you with better services, but also to optimize their products through constant updates." (interviewee 15)*
Accessibility	67%	*"...we have an open Application Programming Interface (API), and we source all relevant IoT databases and integrate them with the ecosystem." (interviewee 9)*
Services	60%	*"The value of IoT lies in the services around it, but in a different way than you would expect. It is no longer about the Service Level Agreement (SLA), but it is about the customer experience." (interviewee 4)*
Domain expertise	53%	*"In my opinion, employing an ISV is an ideal way of overcoming the aforementioned security issues, integration issues, data mining, and knowledge gap. Some ISVs have specific industry or application expertise." (interviewee 15)*
Possibility for updates	40%	*"It is of great value when the functionality increases via software updates." (interviewee 2)*
Security	40%	*"...there is definitely a gap in the market for somebody who solves IoT security issues." (interviewee 12)*

Themes	Percentage of responses	Example quote
Cost reduction	33%	*"The new possibilities of IoT enable us to replace current, old technology, by cheaper alternatives." (interviewee 14)*
Customization	33%	*"...we are adaptable; the fact that we can access our battery separates us from hardware providers, specifically in the beacon market" (interviewee 9)*
Design	33%	*"...much more user experience because of design. Because how else can we make sure that out of the thousands of things devices are capable of, people still discover new things?" (interviewee 10)*
Performance	27%	*"When you are able to let your students make assignments with internet connected pens, then teachers can intervene directly and more efficiently in comparison to the traditional way of making assignments, which involves collecting and checking the results manually and giving feedback the week after." (interviewee 5)*
Newness	27%	*"Thanks to the miniaturization of transmitters and sensors of IoT devices, we now have tons of possibilities to measure new things that we might like to know, so we can collect even more data from our managed assets." (interviewee 14)*

Building block 3. Channels

"Through the web will be the only relevant channel to reach your customers"

In this third building block, something miraculous happened. From all the channels that were mentioned in the original Business Model Canvas, only web sales made it to the next round. Sales force, wholesaler, and own stores were deleted from the list, as none of these channels were mentioned by 25% or more of the interviewees. Although some alternatives were suggested by some of the external experts (word of mouth, apps, cell phones, and beacons), web sales seems to be the preferred channel to reach out for customers who might be interested in IoT. So when selling your IoT services, the experts would rather focus on the virtual world instead of the physical one.

Themes	Percentage of responses	Example quote
Web sales	33%	*"Through the web will be the only relevant channel to reach your customers." (interviewee 4)*

Building block 4. Customer Relationships

"Collaboration and co-creation are the only ways to offer added value at the market place, on any level"

None of the external experts had something to add to the customer relationships building block, instead, they only mentioned three out of six items, which were co-creation, communities, and personal assistance. The items self-service, automated service, and dedicated assistance got removed from the list. What does this tell us? Clearly, automating your communication with customers through IoT applications is not the same as disappearing from view. On the contrary, the experts state that communities, personal assistance and collaboration through co-creation are essential for customer relationships in IoT projects. IoT should not leave your customers hanging by facilitating self-service and automation, but should bridge the gap between companies and customers by bringing them into closer contact with one another. A clear message, when you ask us.

Themes	Percentage of responses	Example quote
Co-creation	53%	*"You have to co-create. That is the only way. Collaboration and co-creation are the only ways to offer added value at the market place, on any level." (interviewee 9)*
Communities	33%	*"We activate the developer community by organizing hackathons and in the App-community we have already organised several meet-ups." (interviewee 10)*
Personal assistance	27%	*"We strive for customer intimacy and put our scarce resources to work as efficiently as possible in order to provide the best service to our customers." (interviewee 3)*

Building block 5. Revenue Streams

"Creating a business that allows other businesses to capitalize on IoT with you, that method is going to be the most successful"

In this fifth building block, massive changes have been made. Usage fees, asset fees, and subscription fees can still be found in the Revised Business Model Canvas, but that is where the resemblance stops. Startup fees, installation fees, brokerage fees: they have all disappeared, just like lending/renting/leasing, licensing, and advertising. Instead, companies working with IoT seem to get their money elsewhere. Prototyping is a newbie that is often mentioned by the external experts (47%) just like the two-sided market, that connects you to another business so you can combine your efforts. Freemium also seems to be a new way of creating revenue streams, as it gets your customers on board by offering a free version of your product before proposing to switch to a more elaborate and payed version.

Themes	Percentage of responses	Example quote
Usage fee	67%	*"We are heading towards a services model, where customers pay for usage." (interviewee 6)*
Subscription fee	47%	*"We want to sell subscriptions to our customers and intermediaries for a few euros a month." (interviewee 1)*
Prototyping/ pilots	47%	*"Organizations are willing to start a pilot, but they are not ready to go all the way with IoT yet." (interviewee 8)*
Two-sided market	47%	*"Creating a business that allows other businesses to capitalize on IoT with you, that method is going to be the most successful." (interviewee 12)*
Leverage customer data	33%	*"We provide free Wi-Fi in the city, only free Wi-Fi does not exist because we pay for it. There will always be something we want in return. That is why we want to collect data from profiles that we can use for commercial opportunities." (interviewee 11)*
Asset sale	27%	*"We started doing large production runs and started selling our beacons to large corporations." (interviewee 9)*
Adoption	27%	*"I would prefer to be paid by the end user based on adoption. If you have so much confidence in your product, you should base a large part based on adoption." (interviewee 7)*
Freemium	27%	*"I am very enthusiastic about open data and open networks. Data must be accessible to everyone and I am quite willing to release data for a trial period or non-commercial usage, but as soon as parties want to receive data based on a data feed structurally, then a price will be charged." (interviewee 11)*

Building block 6. Key Resources

"When you want to combine business with IT, you really need qualified employees that are able to translate the business requirements into sound IT solutions"

So what are the main ingredients of your IoT success mix? The external experts seemed to unanimously agree on employee capabilities. Obviously, you need money and stuff, but there is no way you are going to be successful without the support, expertise, experience, and vision of your co-workers. They are the ones who will translate your brilliant ideas into reality and profitable services, and they are the ones who will communicate with your customers on a regular basis. Therefore, the right human capital is essential for IoT implementation, as we already discussed in chapter 9: Success factor 1. Competences.

Themes	Percentage of responses	Example quote
Employee capabilities	100%	*"The most important resources in IT are the people. When you want to combine business with IT, you really need qualified employees that are able to translate the business requirements into sound IT solutions. You have to have knowledge of IT to be able to understand and explain IT challenges to non-IT people." (interviewee 7)*
Financial resources	53%	*"When we were a start-up, we did not have sufficient financial resources. The cash-out was an important limitation for our projected solutions and that's why we developed a lot ourselves." (interviewee 10)*
Physical resources	33%	*"You have to have sensors that measure everything you want to be measured." (interviewee 14)*

Building block 7. Key Activities

"We are heading towards a situation where we involve more and more suppliers in the design of components for our products"

Key Activities form an essential building block for the IoT business model. It is all about the following: what services will you offer to your customers? The external experts seem to have a clear idea on what are valuable IoT activities. At the top of the list we find platform development, followed by partner management. Information architecture and research and development were added, and the latter is deemed particularly important. As you can see in the table, development and management are important topics to ISVs, since more and more companies want to become interconnected and become able to collect relevant data. Many of them do not know how, and that is where the ISV comes in.

Themes	Percentage of responses	Example quote
Platform development	60%	*"There are organizations emerging that anticipate on the importance of IoT platforms and develop their own platforms to connect other businesses and data feeds." (interviewee 4)*
Partner management	53%	*"We are heading towards a situation where we involve more and more suppliers in the design of components for our products." (interviewee 6)*
Research and development	53%	*"We do a lot of research and product development and come up with solutions without knowing whether the customer wants it or will tender it." (interviewee 11)*
Software development	47%	*"We had to do quite some software development before we were able to utilize the functionality of the beacons. First, we had to adjust our App for detecting and communicating with beacons. Secondly, we had to adjust our back-end systems to translate the signals from the beacon through the App into relevant customer data, and lastly, we had to develop additional web services in order to communicate between our back-end systems and the checkout system." (interviewee 3)*
Sales; marketing	33%	*"Sales and marketing are absolute drivers for IoT. Eventually, you are going to do something with IoT, like increasing prominence as a business or to sell more." (interviewee 4)*
Information architecture	33%	*"Integration of information sources and the ability to collect, store, secure, manage, and provide data. The whole logistic chain of data management must be architected." (interviewee 14)*
Service; implementation	27%	*"Our products include installation and consultancy as well." (interviewee 9)*

Building block 8. Key Partners

"When you have a customer that can help you make things happen, that is when you have a chance of success"

In this eighth building block, a few items have disappeared to make room for a newbie (network providers), a key partner mentioned by the majority of the external experts. Software developers, launching customers, and hardware partners are clearly seen as three very important partners to our external experts, as they were mentioned by nearly half of the interviewees. This is no coincidence, as IoT cannot exist as a standalone application. In order for your company to become successful, you need to get many different people on board to help you with things you simply cannot do by yourself. Moreover, you need partners to provide you with things you do not have, such as a network and hardware, for example.

Themes	Percentage of responses	Example quote
Software developers	47%	*"We tested our iBeacon prototypes together with the developer community and we came up with some really nice user cases." (interviewee 9)*
Launching customers	47%	*"When you have a customer that can help you make things happen, that is when you have a chance of success." (interviewee 12)*
Hardware producers	47%	*"Since we develop hardware we have a manufacturing partner, meaning we do not build the hardware ourselves." (interviewee 10)*
Service partners	40%	*"We approached a partner to install our beacons at all our checkout points and connect them to our network." (interviewee 3)*
Network providers	27%	*"We partnered up with KPN to test the first LoRa beacons." (interviewee 9)*

Building block 9. Cost Structure

"You have to take your ongoing IT costs into account, such as costs for service, security, and push messages"

In this ninth and final building block, many items remained unchanged. Costs for IT, hardware and production, product development, and personnel all appear in both the standard and the revised version of the Business Model Canvas. Marketing, sales costs, and costs for logistics have disappeared however, and they have made room for standardization costs and service costs. Product development is clearly labeled as the most important cost type, followed by costs for IT and hardware/production. This development is far from unexpected, as IoT is all about IT and development and not about logistics. Marketing and sales however are conspicuous by their absence. Does this mean IoT applications speak for themselves and do not need a marketing strategy? We find that hard to believe. The absence of marketing and sales costs may be due to the fact that the many experts were working on internal IoT projects, meaning they did not have to sell or promote anything to their customers.

Themes	Percentage of responses	Example quote
Product development	67%	"The engineering, design and development of our products are a large part of our total costs." (interviewee 6)
IT cost	47%	"You have to take your ongoing IT costs into account, such as costs for service, security, and push messages." (interviewee 8)
Hardware/ production cost	47%	"We currently work with the fourth version of our beacons, and each version had specific functionalities. In the latest version, we managed to solve the battery problem, but we learned our lessons the hard way." (interviewee 9)
Personnel cost	40%	"Our main cost is personnel." (interviewee 10)
Standardization cost	27%	"You standardize your back office processes as much as possible. In the first stage, this is your biggest investment." (interviewee 2)
Service cost	27%	"We pay service costs for our usage." (interviewee 13)

Key business model items for a business in IoT – according to the Yenlo gurus

You now know all about the visions of the external experts we spoke with. Clearly, they have very strong views on what is essential when starting with IoT and what is not. But what about our own experts, the Yenlo gurus that work with different IoT applications on a daily basis? If they do not know what makes a successful IoT business, no one does. Therefore, we will present the IoT business model according to ten of our finest co-workers in this chapter. Below, you will find the Standard Business Model Canvas for IoT applications and the new model that was based on their input.

The Revised Business Model according to the Yenlo gurus

Key Partners	Key Activities	Value Propositions	Customer Relationships	Customer Segments
Launching customers	Platform development	Interoperability	Co-creation	Diversified
Software developers	Software development	Convenience/ usability		
Hardware producers	Sales; marketing	Services		
Service partners	Research and development	Domain expertise		
	Product development	Security		
	Customer development	Accessibility		
	Partner management	Brand/status		

	Key Resources		Channels	
	Employee capabilities		Web sales	
	Financial resources			
	Physical resources			

Cost Structure	Revenue Streams
Personnel cost	Usage fee
Product development cost	Prototyping/pilots
IT cost	Leverage customer data
Marketing & sales cost	Consultancy services
	Two-sided market

Building block 1. Customer Segments

"Our clientele is diversified. There are no constraints."

When we look at customer segments, the Yenlo gurus do not seem to agree with the external experts. Whereas the external experts mainly focus on niche markets, the Yenlo gurus unanimously voted for a diversified strategy. This difference can be well explained by the fact that IoT techniques can be implemented pretty much everywhere, meaning the people who work on implementation processes do not have any constraints when it comes to customer segments. Companies starting with IoT, however, should select their segments more carefully, as their services may not be relevant or useful to specific customer markets.

Themes	Percentage of responses	Example quote
Diversified	100%	*"Our clientele is diversified. There are no constraints." (interviewee 19)*

Building block 2. Value Propositions

"It is all about the service we provide, plus a few things that we have developed on top of our platform to maintain the system"

The original building block on value propositions did not involve domain expertise, services, or security, but was mentioned by both the external experts and the Yenlo gurus. Clearly, specific knowledge and skills are highly needed in the fast growing IoT industry, just as the necessity to protect and secure our networks, programs, and data. One thing the external experts did not mention, was interoperability. The Yenlo gurus did; as a matter of fact, it came up in every single interview. Interoperability seems to be a number one priority for ISV employees, but was not mentioned by the experts actually working on the IoT project. What does this tell us? Is interoperability just not important enough to be mentioned, or is it such a matter of course that most people do not even think about it anymore? We believe the latter is true. To ISVs, interoperability is a main goal, whereas to other companies, it is more of a means. To the external experts, the concept of interoperability is so self-evident, it is not even on top of their minds anymore. The Yenlo gurus, however, look at interoperability from a different angle, since they work on integration on a daily basis.

Themes	Percentage of responses	Example quote
Interoperability	100%	*"Many organizations working with beacons have difficulties integrating their data in their information systems. This is the famous triangle of hardware, mobile apps, and back-end systems. Our added value is that we can solve this triangular problem with our current technical knowhow on interoperability." (interviewee 18)*
Convenience/usability	50%	*"The concept needs to include a benefit for the customer, otherwise he will never become interested. If the threshold is too high, then you will not sell anything." (interviewee 20)*
Services	50%	*"At Yenlo, it is all about the service we provide, plus a few things that we have developed on top of our platform to maintain the system. This is our added value." (interviewee 21)*
Domain expertise	40%	*"You have to develop specific domain knowledge in order to prove your added value." (interviewee 25)*
Security	40%	*"The true power of our solutions lies in security. We make sure that only authorized people get access to the system. Furthermore, we make sure that the authorization level reaches every single beacon. This way you prevent competition to advertise through your beacons." (interviewee 19)*
Accessibility	30%	*"The value of our platform increases as the number of accessible beacons grows. Ultimately, it hinges on the number of beacons that are connected to our platform. The lower the number of beacons that are available on our platform, the less value the platform has to customers." (interviewee 23)*
Brand/status	30%	*"One can recognize us because of our expertise in open source, IoT and interoperability. Our brand revolves around Open source IoT in combination with WSO2." (interviewee 18)*

Building block 3. Channels

"We need to have references so we can share our success stories"

When it comes to selling your products and services, the Yenlo gurus have different ideas on which channels to use. Instead of using the internet to reach customers, they rather focus on conferences, references from satisfied customers, and their own sales team. This different view on channels could be possible due to the fact that an ISV offer is characterized by a particularly elaborate buyer journey, meaning that physical contact (whether at an event or by telephone) is extremely important. Indeed, purchasing an integration platform is not something you do every day; it is an important decision that takes times and careful examination. On the other hand, something simple as a train ticket or a new piece of furniture may be bought online as an impulse buy. Before making any decision on your sales channel, think about the things you offer. Where do your customers go to buy them? Do they shop online, at events, in the street? This is crucial information if you want to reach your target audience.

Themes	Percentage of responses	Example quote
Sales force	60%	*"The sales force is of great importance when you put such an IoT concept to the market." (interviewee 25)*
References	50%	*"We need to have references so we can share our success stories." (interviewee 17)*
Conferences	50%	*"We should attend and be an expert speaker at IoT conferences." (interviewee 20)*

Building block 4. Customer Relationships

"We help our customers with security and maintenance so data information gets managed in the right way"

Now this building block is interesting. Whereas the external experts preferred to reach their customers through either co-creation, communities, or personal assistance, the Yenlo gurus mainly focus on co-creation. This is where ISVs are very different from other vendors, as their services are so renewing and determining for the corporate systems of the client that they cannot do their work without the insights of the people working with them. So instead of dropping off their services and sending an invoice, they enter into close contact with their customers to get to the bottom of their problems and opportunities. Co-creation is nothing to be scared of, as including your customers in the process will only make the implementation and adoption run smoother.

Themes	Percentage of responses	Example quote
Co-creation	80%	*"We are part of the engineering process of our customers and help them with security and maintenance so data information gets managed in the right way." (interviewee 17)*

Building block 5. Revenue Streams

"My revenue is gained by the number of messages that are processed through our platform"

The external experts and the Yenlo gurus agree on many items in this fifth building block on revenue streams. Many of those items are new to the Revised Business Model Canvas, such as prototyping/pilots, leverage customer data, and two-sides market. Usage fees are most popular among all 26 interviewees. Using this type of revenue model is a clever way of benefiting from your customers' success, as you get a part of each click, message, or view. For the Yenlo gurus, prototyping and pilots also play a big part, as they are the perfect way to convince customers of their expertise. Not unexpectedly, leverage customer data is mentioned by 50% of the Yenlo gurus. Indeed, data is IoT's biggest asset, since connecting different systems is all about sharing and interpreting information. The gurus also added consultancy services to the list, which is not surprising given the fact that their knowledge and expertise are one of their strongest cards.

Themes	Percentage of responses	Example quote
Usage fee	90%	*"My revenue is gained by the number of messages that are processed through our platform. This is like a pay per click or a pay per view model." (interviewee 18)*
Prototyping/ pilots	70%	*"It is easy to convince a customer to go on, by doing a pilot project, but you have to monitor that you are not losing on profit." (interviewee 20)*
Leverage customer data	50%	*"The funny thing is that people do not give up their privacy, unless they get something in return, like discounts or gadgets." (interviewee 20)*
Consultancy services	40%	*"Within the closed community of IoT projects you will soon end up in the consulting services." (interviewee 18)*
Two-sided market	40%	*"The APIs on our platform will be provided to developers, so they can build their Apps with our APIs. This means that on the one hand Apps can request an API call to our platform, and on the other hand customers can run campaigns with beacons on our platform." (interviewee 25)*

Building block 6. Key Resources

"You need people that are experts in integration architecture, infrastructure, networks, and anything that is of importance in IoT"

Bingo! There is no building block that the interviewees agree on more than key resources. Pay attention, because what you are about to read is really important. Out of all resources mentioned in the Standard Business Model Canvas, the three key resources that made it to both lists were employee capabilities, financial resources, and physical resources (in that order). Clearly, the success of IoT projects hinges on the expertise, experience, and skills of employees, as no one else is going to do the job for you. Unless your plans and designs are well-structured and carefully executed, IoT will get you nowhere. So if you want to invest in anything, go with human capital. Do not settle for less than brilliancy and ingenuity, you are going to need it.

Themes	Percentage of responses	Example quote
Employee capabilities	100%	*"You need people that are experts in integration architecture, infrastructure, networks, and anything that is of importance in IoT." (interviewee 25)*
Financial resources	50%	*"We always start with the financial part, as that is what we need in order to design and develop any piece of software." (interviewee 23)*
Physical resources	40%	*"IoT is mostly related to physical machinery; physical things have a much longer life span that IT related things." (interviewee 17)*

Building block 7. Key Activities

"We have to invest in building networks, and relationships with customers, and experts upfront"

The seventh building block of the Yenlo gurus is quite similar to the one by the external experts. Platform development is deemed most important to both groups, just as newbie research and development. The latter is an important addition to the Revised Business Model Canvas, as IoT is a broad phenomenon that lacks research or a clear manual. Thus, businesses working with IoT have to go out and collect as much information as possible in order to improve their services. This information is extremely valuable, as it may be the input that is going to set you apart from your competition. In the world of IoT, knowledge is power.

Themes	Percentage of responses	Example quote
Platform development	80%	*"We should be able to develop our platform in a couple of software development iterations resulting in a product that is 50% correct so there is room for another 50% of adjustments."* (interviewee 19)
Software development	70%	*"We develop our own product software."* (interviewee 18)
Sales; marketing	50%	*"Sales is of great importance for IoT product development."* (interviewee 25)
Research and development	50%	*"With R&D we do an early technology feasibility check."* (interviewee 17)
Product development	30%	*"I would like to develop an IoT product to manage beacons through our platform, which we can sell white labelled and as an off the shelf product."* (interviewee 18)
Customer development	30%	*"We have to invest in building networks, and relationships with customers, and experts upfront."* (interviewee 17)
Partner management	30%	*"I think you need to invest time in managing partnerships and customer relations specifically."* (interviewee 20)

Building block 8. Key Partners

"You need to have a launching customer. You can create amazing things, but if there is no customer, you have nothing"

When you ask the Yenlo gurus, a launching customer is the most important key partner when starting an IoT project, closely followed by software partners, and hardware partners. The external experts had the exact same top three, though in a different order. The only thing missing from the list by the Yenlo gurus is the item network providers. Clearly, they are so used to the internet as their communication mode, they do not even think about other options, such as LoRa (Long Range Low Power). Nevertheless, this does not mean that network providers should not be taken into consideration. The construction of your office may seem unimportant to you; when it breaks down, you wish you had taken preventative measures.

Themes	Percentage of responses	Example quote
Launching customers	60%	*"You need to have a launching customer. You can create amazing things, but if there is no customer, you have nothing." (interviewee 19)*
Software developers	50%	*"We have to start a network with partners that are experts in their particular market segment." (interviewee 17)*
Hardware producers	50%	*"You need some partners that build those network devices so you can buy from them." (interviewee 22)*
Service partners	40%	*"You just use services from Amazon, Azure, or Google." (interviewee 24)*

Building block 9. Cost Structure

"Rent a platform in the cloud to start with. I would recommend to start with less servers, so you can add more as the demand starts to grow"

When it comes to cost structure, both expert groups agree on costs for personnel, IT, and product development. Service costs do not occur in the Revised Business Model Canvas of the Yenlo gurus, probably because they themselves are the ones providing the services, eliminating the need to pay for them. Still, the Yenlo gurus do mention the costs for marketing and sales, whereas the external experts did not.

Themes	Percentage of responses	Example quote
Personnel cost	80%	*"You face personnel costs for the development and maintenance of the IoT service." (interviewee21)*
Product development	70%	*"It's unbelievably expensive to build software that can be sold as a product." (interviewee 17)*
Marketing & sales cost	70%	*"Especially in the beginning, sales and marketing will be the biggest items of expense." (interviewee 20)*
IT cost	60%	*"Rent a platform in the cloud to start with. I would recommend to start with less servers, so you can add more as the demand starts to grow." (interviewee 23)*

14. ▸Dealing with IoT challenges

We now have some very useful input to develop a final version of the Business Model Canvas for ISVs working with IoT. But besides key partners, revenue streams, and customer relationship types, a successful IoT implementation hinges on the competences of the ones involved in the process, and their ways of overcoming the challenges that come with IoT technology. So before we head on to our conclusions and recommendations, we need to look into those as well.

Challenges according to the external experts

As we discussed in chapter 8, privacy, security, and technology are the challenges most mentioned in literature. However, since IoT is a new software domain that has not been involved in many studies, we wanted to see for ourselves. This is why we asked our interviewees about these challenges, and they came up with a list of obstacles which have to be taken into account before you should even consider to start with IoT. Below you will find the list by the external experts, with new items in bold.

Challenges according to the external experts
Privacy
Security
Trust
Awareness
Business value
Technology • **Inter-device communication** • Storage • Power management
Legislation
Risk management
Open data

> "A key element of IoT is security. Some companies may not be able to either build or use IoT devices until they know how to solve their security issues"

As was to be expected, privacy and security remain important issues to an IoT related business. Indeed, when sensitive information gets leaked, companies risk being seriously harmed, fined, and let down by their customers. Many discussions about the use of the internet revolve around the usage of personal information, and the online integration, and exchange of data. That is why legislation and risk management are deemed to be important pillars, but the transparency and trustworthiness of ISVs working on IoT should go beyond the principles prescribed by the government. You see, IoT is new to many people, so they might not all get on board that easily. It is thus no surprise that trust is mentioned by 40% of the external experts, as a lack of it may cause serious trouble. Many interviewed experts believe it is not about the actual data that gets shared, but about the confidence customers have in the reliability of data platforms, IT solutions, and service providers. Another remarkable item on the list is technology, that got split into three subjects: inter-device communication, storage, and power management. Wow. This paragraph is getting extremely long, let's have a break here.

The word 'technology' is quite vague and no longer covers the variety of challenges that today's businesses working with IoT face, so more specific descriptions are in place. When working with massive amounts of data, you need to take security measures so you can safely store and quickly move them, hence the need for sufficient storage possibilities. You want to organize your data streams in a way that information can be retrieved anywhere and at any time of day, but only by people and organizations that are authorized. Moreover, you should think about ways to charge your beacons and sensors, as electricity and power points are not always available. Last but not least, turning dreams about IoT into reality may not always be as simple as it seems. A certain business value should always be the fundament, as innovations that do not serve a goal or solve a problem lose all of their legitimacy.

Challenge	Percentage of responses	Example quote
Privacy	87%	*"We don't know to what extent privacy is going to have an impact on the generation that has put their whole life on the internet, because that hasn't really been studied yet. I think the attitude towards privacy is changing, and maybe when it gets abused, then we will change back to more private solutions, or we'll carry on in a much more public way instead." (interviewee 12)*
Security	53%	*"A key element of IoT is security. Some companies may not be able to either build or use IoT devices until they know how to solve their security issues. Security is composed of authentication, authorization, and audit. Each aspect of security is evenly important and requires domain expertise. Many IoT devices are deficient in security and need expert help to produce secure solutions. In many cases, IoT security needs to be combined and integrated with other security systems in corporations." (interviewee 15)*
Trust	40%	*"People don't understand technology, and that is why their first reaction is often a negative one." (interviewee 9)*
Awareness	40%	*"Organizations are not aware of the possibilities that can be realized with IoT." (interviewee 2)*
Business value	33%	*"Many people talk about IoT and just as many people see a lot of opportunities, but they are having a hard time realizing their ideas." (interviewee 11)*
Technology: inter-device communication	27%	*"We challenged ourselves to make the technology stack as fast as possible. Ultimately we were capable to execute the data process in one and a half second. This inter-device communication was challenging because we had to cross many technological layers and therefore make many technological optimizations." (interviewee 3)*
Technology: storage	27%	*"Increasingly important in IoT software is the ability to deal with big data and big data in real-time. Today the demand for real-time big data is massive, just as the demand for big data analyses." (interviewee 12)*
Technology: power management	27%	*"Everything has to do with the battery life of the IoT devices, because connecting to a power point is a great barrier to installation and is also very expensive." (interviewee 9)*
Legislation	27%	*"There are legal and ethical challenges, so even when you have covered everything from a legal perspective, and you took care of processing the data properly, then your actions still might be unacceptable from an ethical perspective." (interviewee 11)*
Risk management	27%	*"Suppliers of IoT applications should co-invest and share business risks with their customers, because it is naive to believe that a customer is willing to take responsibility for all of the risks." (interviewee 7)*
Open data	27%	*"The restriction of available data is a big barrier to business models when those data are not open." (interviewee 9)*

Challenges according to the Yenlo gurus

Challenges according to the Yenlo gurus
Business value
Risk management
Privacy
Security
Data ownership

"We have an idea; we have the technology, but we are looking for a customer"

The Yenlo gurus had a slightly different take on the challenges that arise with IoT. From the long list of challenges by the experts, they only mentioned business value, risk management, privacy, and security. Whereas privacy was seen as a top priority by the external experts, the Yenlo gurus agreed on business value as the most important IoT challenge. It is just like one of the interviewees said: "We have an idea, we have the technology, but we are looking for a customer." Here you see the difference between ISVs and other organizations, as the ones providing the IT solution should always look for companies that use IoT to add value to their products and services. Without this customer, ISVs are just a bunch of technical people, working on innovation without a cause. Risk management is also an important pillar, as ISVs need to make clear agreements with their customers on who can be held responsible in case anything goes wrong or if investments offer no returns. A challenge that was not mentioned by the external experts, was data ownership. This issue is particularly important to ISVs, as they work with billions of messages without really owning any of them. "Who owns the data" is an important question, and you should have the answer before starting anything. Discuss the matter with all of your customers, so you will not risk misusing data without you even realizing it.

Challenge	Percentage of responses	Example quote
Business value	70%	*"We have an idea; we have the technology, but we are looking for a customer." (interviewee 18)*
Risk management	50%	*"As soon as we have contracted a launching customer and we are assured that our part of the investments has been returned, that is sufficient for me to invest. There are many bright people with great ideas employed in our organization, but investing in all these ideas without a customer is like signing your bankruptcy upfront." (interviewee 19)*
Privacy	40%	*"I think that privacy is a great challenge for IoT adoption. There will be people who absolutely do not want that their data is being used for other purposes." (interviewee 20)*
Security	30%	*"Security is a challenge especially with IoT, where users need to agree on sharing the information. There is a location of them, but who knows what kind of Apps will be developed on top of that. So security is a big concern. I will be a big problem if someone gets the data that is of someone else." (interviewee 22)*
Data ownership	30%	*"The ownership of data is difficult and must be arranged with contracts. The contract should include the free usage of the data that you capture on the platform." (interviewee 19)*

▸Key IoT competences

15.

It is all very well knowing the obstacles you are about to face, but it is just as important to have insights into the competences you need to overcome them. In chapter 9, we introduced you to the skills we found in literature. Below, you will find out which skills were mentioned by the external experts and the Yenlo gurus.

Competences according to the external experts

Cognition
Technical skills
Analytical skills
Creative skills
Collaborative skills
Social intelligence

"You have to understand both the physical world and the digital world to come up with simple and valuable solutions"

Before skills, intelligence, and the capacity to effectively communicate, the external experts mentioned cognition as the most important competence. In other words: knowledge is your number one priority when you want to start with IoT. This is probably due to the complex and technical character of the concept, its many features, its endless possibilities, and its lack of a theoretical framework. Thus, you should ask yourself whether you have enough in-house knowledge to get started, or whether you should call in the help of other experts. The same goes for the technical skills of your co-workers, by the way. Sometimes it is better to know your boundaries than to bluff your way into a situation you cannot control. Involving experts to get you going, might even be the smartest thing you have ever done. Collaborative skills and communication were two newbies suggested by the external experts. This is not surprising, since IoT gets you into contact with many different parties, requiring a solid coordination of all your activities.

Competence	Percentage of responses	Example quote
Cognition	67%	*"Being able to understand the complexity of the business requirements, and to be aware that this is a moving target, which influences the product development continuously." (interviewee 7)*
Technical skills	67%	*"Both IoT and IIoT need integration as a critical capability. Experts with technical skills in integration are absolutely required." (interviewee 15)*
Analytic skills	47%	*"I think that an analyst fulfils one of the most important roles in the translation of the business requirements into IoT solutions." (interviewee 8)*
Creativity	40%	*"You have to understand both the physical world and the digital world to come up with simple and valuable solutions." (interviewee 9)*
Collaborative skills	40%	*"I think it is all about collaborative skills, because IoT is mainly about collaborating with multiple stakeholders. Therefore, you need to be able to work with many people from different backgrounds." (interviewee 14)*
Social intelligence	33%	*"We need people with empathy, sensitivity and a passion for their business." (interviewee 5)*

Competences according to the Yenlo gurus

Technical skills

Analytical skills

Creative skills

Cognition

"We need architects, because integration architectures are not designed on the sly"

As you can see in the schedule below, the Yenlo gurus were more specific about the main competences. They highly valued technical skills, which is logical when you look at their professional background. Whereas their customers work on many different business levels, the Yenlo gurus focus on the technical part, meaning they should be the absolute experts in their domain, hence the need for technical skills. Cognition was also mentioned, but was deemed less important, probably because to the Yenlo gurus, cognition and technical skills are part of the same thing: expertise in everything that gets IoT to work.

Competence	Percentage of responses	Example quote
Technical skills	90%	"We need technical skills to become experts in utilizing the different generic IoT platforms in order to make tailor made solutions for our clients." (interviewee 17)
Analytic skills	60%	"We need architects, because integration architectures are not designed on the sly. (interviewee 21)
Creativity	40%	"You also need some creative minds that will monitor the entire process, because it is hard to predict all the things that can be achieved with such networks." (interviewee 22)
Cognition	30%	"You need to know the theoretical background and you need to have the capacity to turn theory into practical solutions for customers." (interviewee 25)

▸ The ultimate answers

16.

We reckon that this was a lot of input to progress. Luckily for you, this is the chapter where it all comes together. Here, we will assemble all the puzzle pieces we found and turn them into a clear overview of all the things you need to start your own business in IoT. In chapter 5, we asked ourselves four ultimate IoT related questions. Now, let us give you the ultimate answers.

How can ISVs prepare for tomorrow's business in IoT?

What software architecture do they need as a basis?

Which challenges do they have to take into account?

Which competences are essential for their employees?

Which business model items are relevant?

The ultimate IoT software architecture

An IoT solution incorporates a combination of software products, enabling communication between the Internet and Things. As Paul Fremantle pointed out in chapter 7, there is no step-to-step plan to structure these products, since IoT projects are simply too diverse. This is why he introduced the IoT reference architecture, a framework that you can use to organize and structure your products, no matter what IoT project you are on. You probably wonder what that looks like in real life. This is why, in the picture below[32], we show you how we use the reference architecture for our IoT solutions by running the software products by WSO2 in the cloud. As you can see, the products combined form an architecture that complies with all the criteria Paul mentioned in chapter 7. Sure, we still need to come up with different strategies per customer in order to execute their brilliant but crazy ideas, but this architecture is the framework that gets us started. Do you have all the ingredients that are needed to make a similar architecture for your own company? If the answer is yes: go you! If the answer is no, you might want to consider extending your product portfolio. Given the challenges that come with IoT, you are going to need every single element that we discussed.

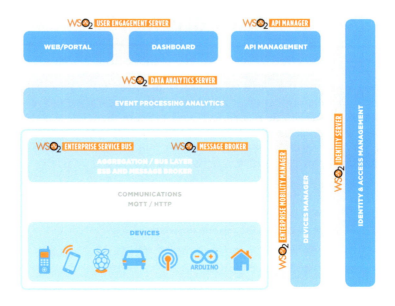

The ultimate IoT challenges

Speaking of challenges, we combined the answers of all our interviewees, resulting in a list of things you should take into account when starting any IoT adventure:

Challenge	Mentioned by % of the interviewees
Privacy	68%
Business value	48%
Security	44%
Awareness	24%
Technology: inter-device communication	16%
Technology: power management	16%

As you can see, privacy will probably be your biggest obstacle. In the end, lawsuits, unethical usage of data, customer mistrust, and public scandals will push you over the edge and will destroy your company's bright future. So in order to tackle the privacy issue, do not take any risks in this area. Board up your security measures and make sure that unauthorized persons have no access to your greatest good, which is your (customers) data. We know it is a cliché, but better safe than -really- sorry. Furthermore, do not underestimate the importance of your business value. As you read in the introduction, good ideas are not enough, nor is technology. Your idea needs to make sense to the end-users, since your success will depend on their satisfaction. Make sure your solution is workable and your technology serves a clear end goal. Both should be in order for you to become successful in IoT.

The ultimate IoT competences

Every business needs competences, but businesses working with IoT should possess specifically skilled and experienced employees. We combined the answers of all our interviewees and created this list of indispensable IoT competences.

Competence	Mentioned by % of the interviewees
Technical skills	76%
Cognition	52%
Analytic skills	52%
Creativity	40%
Collaborative skills	24%
Social intelligence	20%

When putting together your very own IoT team, technical skills are your main focus. Hiring team members with insufficient technical knowledge is like running a Michelin Star restaurant without skilled chefs. At the same time, do not fixate on technical skills alone. IoT requires people to be analytical, creative, collaborative, and -very important- socially intelligent. Technical as they may be, IoT applications are built to make lives less complicated and more comfortable. Thus, empathy and ingenuity should be on top of your wish list. In a perfect world, your team consists of employees who complement each other rather than employees who are interchangeable. This way, you create an out-of-the-box setting, in which your team will thrive on its diversity. A programmer will look at IoT from a different angle than an architect, who will in turn have another view on the process compared to a business analyst.

The ultimate IoT Business Model

Below, you find the most important table of this book: the ultimate business model for ISVs starting with IoT. Having combined the answers given by the external experts and the Yenlo gurus, this is what the Revised Business Model Canvas looks like:

Key Partners	Key Activities	Value Propositions	Customer Relationships	Customer Segments
Launching customers	Platform development	Convenience/ usability	Co-creation	Diversified
Software developers	Software development	Services	Communities	Niche market
Hardware producers	Research & Development	Accessibility		Mass market
Service partners	Partner management	Domain expertise		Segmented
Network providers	Sales; marketing	Comfort		
	Information architecture	Security		
	Service; implementation	Interoperability		
	Product development	Possibilities for updates		
	Customer development	Performance		

	Key Resources		Channels	
	Employee capabilities		Sales force	
	Financial resources		References	
	Physical resources		Conferences	
	Software		Web sales	

Cost Structure		Revenue Streams	
Product development cost		Usage fee	
Personnel cost		Prototyping/pilots	
IT cost		Two-sided market	
Hardware/production cost		Leverage customer data	
Marketing & sales cost		Subscription fees	
Standardization cost		Freemium	

Grocery list

Treat this Revised Business Model Canvas as it was your grocery list. Collect your shopping cart and look at each single building block: what did you already cover and what is still left to do? Did you already take standardization costs into account, are you connected to a potential launching customer, are you engaged in customer communities? And do you have sufficient financial resources, do your employees know their software? By crossing the key business model items off your list, you take a systematic approach in building your IoT oriented business, meaning you lower your risk of falling down the traps we discussed. At the same time, do not fixate on getting every single business model item right. The Business Model Canvas may be a great guideline; it cannot tell you when you are ready to get started. You know your company best, so you will be the one giving the green light. Are you having trouble figuring out where to start? We suggest you focus on the key business model items that were most mentioned by the interviewees:

• Customer Segments; Diversified
• Value Propositions; Convenience/usability
• Channels; Sales force
• Customer Relationships; Co-creation
• Revenue Streams; Usage fee
• Key Resources; Employee capabilities
• Key Activities; Platform development
• Key Partners; Launching customers
• Cost Structure; Product development cost

Toolbox

So there you have it: a toolbox filled with competences, knowledge of IoT pitfalls, a reference architecture, and key business model items. It is now up to you to use these tools and get your own IoT business on track. In the next chapter, we will send you on your way with our best pieces of advice.

17. ▸ Let's talk business –
recommendations by the author

While creating this book, I have always used the word 'we', as developing it was a team effort. Reading through the conclusion section, however, I felt the book needed something more; a practical chapter giving you some guidance and hands-on advice. It is all very well knowing what you need to get started; getting started is just as important. While writing the thesis that later would form the basis of this book, I realized I had found two matters that should be prioritized by every business starting with IoT, and they seemed like a great starting point to me. So based on what I learnt from writing this book, I give you my piece of advice.

Focus on interoperability and call it convenience

Regarding the value proposition, the majority of the Yenlo gurus stick with interoperability. I would however recommend not to sell interoperability, but to use it as a distinctive advantage when promoting your IoT services. Nevertheless, the external experts did not mention interoperability at all but highly valued convenience and usability instead. What does this conclusion tell us? The most important lesson I learnt is that your value proposition should be about the IoT services you offer to the end-customer. So in order to make your IoT business a success, you need to excel in interoperability so you can offer just that. Although the nature of your IoT service will be technology oriented, try to focus on how the end-user should use it and how easy his life will become. Do not forget about performance either: before anything else, your solution should run flawlessly. By doing all of this, you offer value through interoperability, but you call it convenience instead.

Partner up!

If you want to put in place all the puzzle pieces of your IoT architecture, you need partners. Many experts mentioned the importance of a launching partner, which is a customer that you have worked with for a while and who wants to co-create your ideas. Together, you should figure out a way the aforementioned convenience to the end-customer, rather than deploying new systems for the sake of innovation. A launching customer will enable you to do a pilot before you jump into the deep end, so you have some time to learn from your mistakes. Furthermore, you will need to partner up with your own co-workers. According to a majority of the interviewees, employee capabilities are your greatest good, since their technical and collaborative (there is the word again) skills, creativity, and social intelligence will make your IoT dream team. Apart from a launching partner and your own team, you will need help from other companies that do something completely different, in order for you to get the best out of every single component of your solution. Tesla, for example, could never do what Spotify does, and vice versa. Why would they even want to, when they can join forces? Last but not least, there are the outside partners that will be connected to your platforms, adding applications to your systems, and optimizing your processes (hence the need for API management, see chapter 7). To summarize: you need to collaborate whenever you can, wherever you can.

You did it!

You have come to the end of the story. Or at least to the end of this book, because hopefully, this will be your starting point. We have shared our knowledge and study findings, and now it is all up to you. Take our advice and start gathering the right people, keep in mind the pitfalls and focus on convenience through interoperability. In a couple of months, you will hear yourself say: "This is it, we did it!" The sensors will work and the devices will be in place. All that you will have to do, is to switch them on.

Good luck!

René Wiersma
Enterprise Architect at Yenlo

"In the world of
IoT, knowledge
is power"

▸About Yenlo

Yenlo is a group of smart people who support organizations in making their IT systems fast and agile. We unravel and we connect, so that data streams flow within companies, between companies, to customers, and back to you. We are proud partners of WSO2, we offer flexible open source solutions, and we make sure our services are both API and IoT centric. Hence, the sky is not a limit.

In our Yenlo LABS department we constantly work on innovative projects. We collaborate as much as we can, in order to get the very best out of our solutions. We believe that everyone is capable of doing great things, as long as they have access to the right tools and professionals. This is why we offer both.

The Yenlo gurus know what it takes to get even the most complex IT projects off the ground. At the same time, we keep you up-to-date with our white papers, webinars, and training sessions.
Do you want to know more about us and our products, or do you want a nice talk about IoT with one of our experts? Just say the word!

www.yenlo.com
info@yenlo.com

19. ▸About the author

René Wiersma MSc MBA is Enterprise Architect at Yenlo and has more than 15 years of experience in helping organizations designing and implementing strategic and operational business and IT solutions.

With an MBA degree in Business & IT, a Master's degree in Enterprise Architecture, and a long history in programming, he has built expertise in both business and technology, which enables him to easily shift from exploring strategic opportunities with board members to exploring technological features with developers.

René has always been fascinated by the way technology changes society and closely monitors the development of IoT. Being a techie, he cannot help wanting to find out everything there is to know about new IT strategies, enterprise engineering, customer trends and the way they collide. René is married and father of two, and he lives in Wageningen, the Netherlands.

René Wiersma MSc MBA
Enterprise Architect at Yenlo

▶ Words you need

20.

API Application Programming Interface that enables communication between systems, devices, and beacons.

Beacons Small devices transmitting the whereabouts of people through Bluetooth Low Energy (BLE). Built-in beacons can be found in smartphones and computers. They are often provided with a battery but can also be plugged into an USB port.

IoT Internet of Things. Further explained in chapter 6.

ISV Independent Software Vendor. Businesses that develop and sell enterprise software.

Open source software Software that is publicly accessible so that external developers can modify the products and contribute to their optimization. Open source revolves around communities, participation, and transparency.

SLA Service Level Agreement. A document containing information about the products and services that are part of the contract between a supplier and a customer.

WSO2 WSO2 is an international software company that offers middleware solutions to customers. Being 100% open source, cloud ready, and scalable, their enterprise platform is used by many preeminent companies all over the world. Well-known products are the WSO2 ESB and WSO2 API management.

Yenlo Yours truly.

---

56 **Wat is ERP?** http://www.erpsystemen.nl/wat-is-erp

21. ▶Bibliography

ABN Amro (2016). **Industrial Internet of Things: Noodzaak voor Industrie, kans voor IT-sector,** ABN Amro Insights.

Afshar, V. (2014, May 29). **14 Google Glass Innovative Uses In Education.** Retrieved May 28, 2016, from http://www.huffingtonpost.com/vala-afshar/14-google-glass-innovativ_b_5410893.html

Albrecht, K. (2008). **How RFID Tags Could Be Used to Track Unsuspecting People.** Scientific American, September. Retrieved May 10, 2016, from

http://www.scientificamerican.com/article/how-rfid-tags-could-be-used/

Amsterdam iBeacon Living Lab. Retrieved November 1, 2015, from iBeacon Living Lab: http://ibeaconlivinglab.com/ For more information on LoRa, see the LoRa Alliance website: https://www.lora-alliance.org/

Andersson, P., & Mattsson, L. (2015). **Service Innovations Enabled by the "Internet of Things".** IMP Journal, 9 (1), 85-106.

Ashton, K. (2009). **That "Internet of Things" Thing.** RFiD Journal.

Atzori, L., Iera, A., & Morabito, G. (2010). **The Internet of Things: A Survey.** Computer Networks.

Balamuralidhar, P., Prateep, M., & Arpan, P. (2013). **Software Platforms for Internet of Things and M2M**. Journal of the Indian Institute of Science, 93 (3), 487-497.

Brisbourne, A. (n.d.). **Tesla's Over-the-Air Fix: Best Example Yet of the Internet of Things?** Retrieved May 15, 2016, from

http://www.wired.com/insights/2014/02/teslas-air-fix-best-example-yet-internet-things/

Chan, H. (2015). **Internet of Things Business Models**. Journal of Service Science and Management, 8, 552-568.

Dijkman, R., Sprenkels, B., Peeters, T., & Janssen, A. (2015). **Business Models for the Internet of Things.** International Journal of Information Management, 35, 672-678.

Efremov, S., Pilipenko, N., & Voskov, L. (2015). **An Integrated Approach to Common Problems in the Internet of Things.** 25th DAAAM International Symposium on Intelligent

Fremantle, P. (2015). **A Reference Architecture for the Internet of Things**. WSO2.

Fremantle, P., Aziz, B., Kopecký, J., & Scott, P. (2014). **Federated Identity and Access Management for the Internet of Things.** 3rd International Workshop on the Secure IoT (pp. 10-17). Wroclaw: IEEE.

Fried, L. (2014, May 15). **A Bill of Rights for the Internet of Things**. Retrieved January 30, 2016, from The New York Times: http://www.nytimes.com/roomfordebate/2013/09/08/privacy-and-the-internet-of-things/a-bill-of-rights-for-the-internet-of-things

Gartner. (n.d.). **Gartner Hype Cycle**. Retrieved May 27, 2016, from http://www.gartner.com/technology/research/methodologies/hype-cycle.jsp

Gassmann, O., Frankenberger, K., & Csik, M. (2014). **Revolutionizing the Business Model.**

In Management of the Fuzzy Front End of Innovation (pp. 89-97). Springer International Publishing.

Gassmann, O., Frankenberger, K., & Csik, M. (2014). **The Business Model Navigator.** Harlow: Pearson.

Gubbi, J., Buyya, R., Marusic, S., & Palaniswami, M. (2013). **Internet of Things (IoT): A Vision, Architectural Elements, and Future Directions.** Future Generation Computer Systems, 29, 1645-1660.

Hackers Caused Power Cut in Western Ukraine - US. (2016, January 12). Retrieved June 24, 2016, from http://www.bbc.co.uk/news/technology-35297464

iBeaconinfo. (2015, July 16). **Schiphol heeft bijna 2000 beacons geplaatst.** Retrieved November 1, 2015, from iBeaconinfo: http://ibeaconinfo.nl/schiphol-heeft-bijna-2000-beacons-geplaatst/

Lee, I., & Lee, K. (2015). **The Internet of Things (IoT): Applications, Investments, and Challenges for Enterprises.** Business Horizons, 58, 431-440.

Lin, M., Li, S., & Whinston, A. (2011). **Innovation and Price Competition in a Two-Sided Market.** Journal of Information Systems Management, 28 (2), 171-202.

Mahadevan, B. (2000). **Business Models for Internet-Based E-commerce: An Anatomy.** California management review, 42 (4), 55-69.

Mathon, J. (2013, November 8). **Inner Source, Open source for the Enterprise.** Retrieved April 26, 2016, from CloudRamblings: https://cloudramblings.me/2013/11/08/inner-source-open-source-for-the-enterprise/

Mathon, J. (2015, June 22). **What Is the Difference Between Services, Device, Apps, APIs and Microservices.** Retrieved April 30, 2016, from CloudRamblings: https://cloudramblings.me/2015/06/22/services-micro-services-devices-apps-apis-whats-the-difference/

Mathon, J. (2015, September 8). **Security and Privacy – Not the Staid and Boring Business of the Past 20 Years.** Retrieved February 6, 2016, from CloudRamblings: http://cloudramblings.me/2015/09/08/security-and-privacy-not-the-staid-and-boring-business-of-the-past-20-years/

Miorandi, D., Sicari, S., De Pellegrini, F., & Chlamtac, I. (2012). **Internet of things: Vision, Applications and Research Challenges.** Ad Hoc Networks, 10 (7), 1497–1516.

Osterwalder, A., & Pigneur, Y. (2002). **An E-business Model Ontology for Modeling E-business.** 15th Bled Electronic Commerce Conference.

Packard, H. (2014, July 29). **HP Study Reveals 70 Percent of Internet of Things Devices Vulnerable to Attack.** Opgeroepen op Februari 6, 2016, van http://www8.hp.com/us/en/hp-news/press-release.html?id=1744676#.VrZNR4-cFR0

Popp, K., & Meyer, R. (2010). **Profit from Software Ecosystems: Business Models, Ecosystems and Partnerships in the Software Industry.** Books on Demand.

Present Day Dilemmas and Problems - Dutch Farm Experience. (n.d.). Retrieved June 03, 2016, from http://www.dutchfarmexperience.com/present-day-dillemas-problems/

Quby. (n.d.). **Smart Thermostat.** Retrieved April 02, 2016, from http://quby.com/en/page/62

Renck, R., Kahn, E., & Gardner, B. (1969). **Continuing Education in R&D Careers.** DSF Report 69-20, Prepared by the Social Research, Inc.

Rouw, A. (2016). **Human Resource Practices to Prepare for Robots in the Corporate World.** Breukelen: Nyenrode Business Universiteit.

Sicari, S., Rizzardi, A., Grieco, L., & Coen-Porisini, A. (2015). **Security, Privacy and Trust in Internet of Things: The Road Ahead.** Computer Networks (76), 146–164.

Smart Farming (Slim boeren). (n.d.). Retrieved June 03, 2016, from http://www. dairycampus.nl/nl/Home/Expertisegebieden/Smart-Farming.htm

Teece, D. (2010). **Business model, Business Strategy and Innovation.** Long Range Plan, 43 (2-3), 172-194.

Uckelmann, D., Harrison, M., & Michahelles, F. (2011). **Architecting the Internet of Things.** Springer. Van Engeldorp Gastelaars, P. (1998). Theorievorming en methoden van onderzoek binnen de sociale wetenschappen. Nieuwerkerk aan den IJssel: ServicePost B.V.

Vermesan, O., Friess, P., Guillemin, P., Gusmeroli, S., Sundmaeker, H., Bassi, A., et al. (2009). **Internet of Things Strategic Research Roadmap.** Cluster of European Research Projects on the Internet of Things, CERP-IoT.

Waltzman, H., & Shen, L. (2015). **The Internet of Things.** Intellectual Property & Technology Law Journal, 27 (7), 19-21.

Weber, R. (2010). **Internet of Things – New security and Privacy Challenges.** Internet of Things – New Security and Privacy Challenges, 26 (1), 23-30.

Wielen, G., Van der. (2016, February 5). **Interview with IoT experts** [Interview by R. Wiersma].

WSO2 (2014, February 13). **How Boeing Transformed Commercial Aviation Using WSO2** [Weblog post]. Retrieved March 20, 2016, from

http://wso2.com/blogs/thesource/2014/02/wso2con-insights-how-boeing-transformed-commercial-aviation-using-wso2/

www.ingramcontent.com/pod-product-compliance
Lightning Source LLC
Chambersburg PA
CBHW041143050326
40689CB00001B/458